W9-BXQ-750

Next Week, Swan Lake

REFLECTIONS ON DANCE AND DANCES

Maya Plisetskaya as Odette in *Swan Lake*. *Photo by Vladimir Bliokh.*

Next Week, Swan Lake

REFLECTIONS ON DANCE AND DANCES

Selma Jeanne Cohen

WESLEYAN UNIVERSITY PRESS
Middletown, Connecticut

Copyright © 1982 by Selma Jeanne Cohen
All rights reserved.

Lines from "Among School Children": Reprinted with
permission of Macmillan Publishing Co., Inc., from
Collected Poems by William Butler Yeats. Copyright ©
1928 by Macmillan Publishing Co., Inc., renewed 1956
by Bertha Georgie Yeats.
Lines from "Michael Robartes and the Dancer":
Reprinted with permission of Macmillan Publishing Co.,
Inc., from *Collected Poems* by William Butler Yeats.
Copyright © 1924 by Macmillan Publishing Co., Inc.,
renewed 1952 by Bertha Georgie Yeats.
Lines from "The Double Vision of Michael Robartes"
and "The Wild Swans at Coole": Reprinted with
permission of Macmillan Publishing Co., Inc., from
Collected Poems by William Butler Yeats. Copyright ©
1919 by Macmillan Publishing Co., Inc., renewed 1947
by Bertha Georgie Yeats.

All inquiries and permissions requests should be
addressed to the Publisher, Wesleyan University Press,
110 Mt. Vernon Street, Middletown, Connecticut 06457

Distributed by Harper & Row Publishers, Keystone
Industrial Park, Scranton, Pennsylvania 18512

Library of Congress Cataloging in Publication Data

Cohen, Selma Jeanne, 1920–
    Next week, Swan Lake.

    Bibliography: p.
    Includes index.
    1. Dancing—Addresses, essays, lectures.   2. Dancing
—Philosophy—Addresses, essays, lectures.   I. Title.
GV 1599.C64   793.3   82-2614 AACR2
ISBN 0-8195-6110-X

Manufactured in the United States of America

First printing, 1982
Wesleyan Paperback, 1986

*This book is dedicated
to the memory of*
BILL BUENO

Preface

THE LATE Harold Rosenberg once said of the visual arts that "in dealing with *new* things there is a question that precedes that of good or bad. I refer to the question 'What is it?'—the question of identity." I agree with this, but—perhaps because I am a historian—I would like to see it extended to apply to the old as well as to the new. Granting that the major dance innovators of recent times have met with more than their share of intolerant critics, we have also seen traditional choreography subjected to some equally prejudiced notices. Both extremes, it seems to me, stem from thinking that all dance can be perceived in the same way, that standards of right and wrong are identical for all dances, even when their utterly distinctive styles should warn the observer that similarly distinctive criteria may be in order. Because such a straitjacket approach tends to lead to the dismissal of whatever does not fit the predetermined formula, it closes the eyes to many delights. What a pity!

Categories can be useful when they provide a context for viewing, but they can be dangerous when they tempt us into exaggerated generalizations. I do not believe that all contemporary western dance can be divided into two parts: ballet and modern. I struggled with this for some years, demonstrating the problem to my students by asking, "Where do we put Twyla Tharp?" Now the forthcoming international encyclopedia of dance will put our anxieties to rest; she goes under "T."

Today we are confronted not only with a fantastic variety of annual creations but also—thanks to the more extensive use of notation and film—with a growing repertory of works from the past. We frequently now refer to the emergence of the versatile dancer—the one who can perform in works by both Marius Petipa and Doris Humphrey with appropriate feeling and attack for each. We might also consider the desirability of cultivating the versatile audience, one that will adjust its sights to the work at hand, not wishing always that it were either more comfortably familiar or more provocatively avant-garde, but welcoming each opportunity to challenge the perception and enrich the sensibility. Judgment can come later.

This book is concerned with questions of identity: the identity of particular works, of genres, of dance itself. *Swan Lake* is only an illustration, though it happens to be an especially convenient one as it exemplifies so many of the problems—historic, dramatic, stylistic, personal—that make this art so challenging. I will concentrate on western theatrical concert dance, not because I feel that other kinds are less valid or less interesting, but because I find the issues raised by this one so rich and complex and intriguing that I am reluctant to risk slighting its complexities in order to cover a broader field.

"What kind of a book is it?" some friends asked. History? There is historical material in it, but the problems considered are not historical, not matters of establishing date or place, of analyzing a personality or recreating a period ambience. Philosophy? The problems are fundamental to the philosophy of art, questions of ontology, epistemology, and hermeneutics. But I have not limited the discussion to matters of theory; rather, I have dealt extensively with particular dances, both historic and contemporary. Contemporary? Then perhaps it is a book of criticism! But I have not restricted the subject to contemporary works and besides I have drawn on the writings of a number of aestheticians. Perhaps the question had best be left unanswered. I am grateful to Peter Kivy for calling my attention to Whitehead's remark that the universe is not divided into departments.

This is a book about dance and ideas about dance. The ideas are simply ones that have, over the years, intrigued me. Some were prompted by readings in criticism and philosophy, some by attendance at performances. It happens that I enjoy both, feeling that the pleasure I take in one is enhanced by my delight in the other. While it may be amusing to construct theories that refer to some imaginary form of human movement, I prefer to look for ideas that illuminate the art as we actually experience it. Dance does not take place in the mind (though I admit I have choreographed some magnificent ballets there), but on the stage. Thinking about dance may be a means to an end that is not only a conceptual scheme but an enriched theatrical experience.

One such experience could be of *Swan Lake*.

Acknowledgments

IT WAS THE University of Chicago that taught me to be a pluralist, though its English Department expected me to apply that range of appreciation to poems rather than dances. I remain deeply grateful for the training in neo-Aristotelian analysis, while confessing my somewhat idiosyncratic uses of it.

My first published article on dance appeared in the *Journal of Aesthetics and Art Criticism,* and its sponsoring organization, the American Society for Aesthetics, has been a source of inspiration and support to me ever since. Its founder, the late Thomas Munro, was among the first to encourage my work with dance. Later society officers Rudolf Arnheim, Arnold Berleant, Monroe Beardsley, and Herbert Schueller supplied me with germs of ideas and occasions to develop them. Additional encouragement and opportunities were provided by the American Society for Theatre Research, especially by William Green.

Unwitting assistance came from those intrepid inquirers, the students who survived my exploratory courses in dance aesthetics at the Five College Consortium of Amherst, Hampshire, Mount Holyoke, Smith, and the University of Massachusetts, as well as at Dance Theatre Workshop in New York. York University in Toronto, along with the universities of Illinois and Wisconsin, let me try out some of these ideas in weekend seminars.

This book actually began with the assistance of a grant from the John Simon Guggenheim Memorial Foundation. Then The New York Public Library provided me with dusty volumes, long buried in its west-side annex and full of fascinating treasures. The Dance Collection of the Library and Museum of Performing Arts at Lincoln Center added its unique assemblage of books, films, and valuable ephemera.

For leading me to unsuspected sources of information and assisting with suggestions historical, philosophical, and technical, I am indebted to Susan Au, Curtis Carter, Arlene Croce, George Dorris, Jack Glickman, Els Grelinger, Ann and Ivor Guest, Joel Honig, Anna Kisselgoff, Vera Krasovskaya, Patricia McAndrew, Joseph Margolis, Genevieve Oswald, Herta Pauly, and David Vaughan. Chapter 6 is for Bernard L. Koten. Special thanks to Edward Gorey for unwittingly illustrating the theme of this book.

Chapter 5 was published in somewhat different form in *Dance Chronicle*. A number of ideas developed here first appeared in various articles and reviews in *Dance Magazine, Dance Research Journal,* and the *Journal of Aesthetics and Art Criticism*.

Contents

List of Illustrations

1. *The Problems of* SWAN LAKE

"You can be Benno, the Prince's Friend, and catch me just before I hit the floor."

Drawing by Edward Gorey. From The Lavender Leotard *(New York: Gotham Book Mart, 1973).*

So YOU ARE going to see *Swan Lake*, the great and long-admired classic. I hope you enjoy it. But what, precisely, are you going to see?

Swan Lake, first produced in Moscow in 1877 with choreography by Julius Wenzel Reisinger and music by Peter Ilyich Tchaikovsky, was dropped from the repertory of the Bolshoi Theatre after five years of apparently mediocre productions. By that time, however, a variety of attempts had been made to rescue it from impending oblivion. The notices had not been all that bad; perhaps it could be saved. Even within the first season, Marius Petipa had composed a new pas de deux for the third act, and Ludwig Minkus had written new music for it. An assortment of interpolations and substitutions from other ballets followed, while Joseph Hansen made revisions of his own for the productions he staged in Moscow in 1880 and 1882.

When Petipa set out to rechoreograph the entire ballet in St. Petersburg in 1894, he was already seventy-six years old and busy; consequently he assigned part of the job to his assistant Lev Ivanov, who had staged a new version of the second act earlier that year for a memorial program dedicated to Tchaikovsky. Ivanov choreographed the final act, thus taking responsibility for the lyrical episodes in the story of Odette, the princess who has been enchanted by the evil Rothbart and is doomed to the life of a swan unless Prince Siegfried fulfills his pledge of fidelity. Petipa retained for himself the choreography for the first act, which introduces the prince, and for most of the technically brilliant third act, in which Siegfried is seduced by the pretender Odile into betraying his beloved and bringing about the tragic ending.

This is the famous *Swan Lake* of 1895, the one to which most contemporary programs refer, though often with the stipulation that the choreography is "after" Petipa and Ivanov. How much "after" is an intriguing question, for anyone who has seen even two productions is aware that, although the program notes may be identical, the ballets are not. Recognizable probably, possibly even quite similar, but never exactly the same. The deviations may be minor—just an extra bar of chainé turns here or there, a slower tempo perhaps. Or they may be substantial: a solo or ensemble added or omitted or augmented with some unfamiliar steps; new characters introduced or familiar ones dropped.

Because *Swan Lake* can be experienced only in performance, what the audience encounters each time is a realization of—of what? The intentions of the choreographer? How do we know them? No conveniently detailed diaries provide this information. From the notated score of the dance? Most often, for works created prior to this century, there is no such score, but it happens that for *Swan Lake* there is one. Or rather, there are several. Which only complicates the problem.

Nicholas Sergeyev brought scores of the choreography of *Swan Lake* from Russia and used them for the production that was staged by the Vic-Wells Ballet in London in 1934. To Sergeyev, the scores were simply aids to memory, since he already knew the work. His manuscripts, now in the Harvard Theatre Collection, contain directions for twenty-three dances from the Petipa-Ivanov *Swan Lake*, providing a virtually complete record of their steps and floor plans, but no indications of arm or body movements and no corresponding music. Obviously, these twenty-three dances constitute only portions of the complete ballet. Even more important: the notations do not date from a single year, but seem to have been written over a period during which a number of changes were made in the production. We have evidence for some of the alterations. In the years between the Moscow premiere and the St. Petersburg production, for example, we know that the first two acts were made into one act with two scenes, and that several dances were lifted out of one act and dropped into another. Within the following ten years several new variations were introduced by Mathilde Kschessinskaya, who first took over the role of the heroine from Pierina Legnani in 1901. We also know that the prince's friend, Benno, used by Petipa in the adagio of act 1, scene 2, was omitted from some later productions but was subsequently reinstated (today he is usually banished again). The ordering of the national dances in the second act was altered frequently.

Why were these changes made? They are hardly explicable on artistic grounds; in fact, they seem quite arbitrary. Placed in their historical context, however, they make perfect sense. The amalgamation of the first two acts kept the audience from getting restless by having the leading ballerina, the Odette/Odile of the evening, appear before first intermission. The St. Petersburg ballet-goers wanted her sooner and they made sure that their wishes were known. The matter of Benno's appearance in the adagio was due to an equally practical reason of a different sort: the aging Paul Gerdt found it physically too difficult to handle the partnering. Still, seniority entitled him to the role of the hero, so an adjustment had to be made.

Petipa's notes for *Swan Lake*, insofar as they are known to us outside Russia, deal exclusively with details: the color of the flowers in the girls' baskets, which dancer would perform what. There is no evidence of his considering the relevance of these details to a structural entity, of making a change in order to intensify a dramatic situation or to provide contrast in a succession of scenes. He was a practical man of the theatre, less concerned with the integrity of his art work than with what the budget would allow, what would please the tsar, and what would sell tickets. In spite of this attitude he created works that possessed the very artistic qualities that were apparently of so little conscious importance to him. But, of necessity, his mind was attuned to matters of expediency, and such has been the case of his successors as well, for they too have modified and adjusted their ballet productions to accommodate the particular resources at their disposal.

Since Petipa's time, *Swan Lake* has continued to evolve to such an extent that John Wiley has suggested calling it a "work in progress." Many of the subsequent changes can be accounted for by variations in material circumstances, for few of the productions that followed enjoyed resources as luxurious as those of St. Petersburg's Maryinsky Theatre. Most often fewer swans were available for the corps and less spectacular scenic effects had to suffice. Ethical and political climates were also influential, affecting the more or less sympathetic view of the royal family or the attitude toward the lack of moral justice in the tragic ending. But the crucial factor has been the one that ballet shares with other performing arts—the changing nature of the personalities who bring it to life on the stage.

Our contemporary attitude, fostered by the current accessibility of recording devices, tends to honor the identity of the dance work in a manner that might have astonished both the creators and the audience of the St. Petersburg *Swan Lake*. To a nineteenth-century producer, a ballet was not at all an inviolable treasure; on the contrary, he seemed to consider it primarily as a commodity, an item, to be spruced up occasionally for marketing to an audience more interested in novelty than in an "authentic," historically oriented reproduction of the sensation of a previous decade. While (sometimes) maintaining a basic plot line, the director entrusted with the revival quite often added some dance numbers of his own devising, threw out old ones, made various adjustments to show off the brilliance of a new star or to hide the weaknesses of an old one who refused to quit the scene. A ballet was primarily a vehicle designed to exploit something beyond itself—most frequently the latest star, but it could also be a newly fashionable interest in ancient Egypt, or a recently constructed lakeside theatre on the estate of a prominent aristocrat.

While the contemporary audience recognizes the work as an entity, it accepts revised stagings and often even considers their freshness a major attraction. A modernized variation for the ballerina, like a refurbished decor, may alert us to values in the work that have been dimmed by time and overfamiliarity, a fact that enterprising companies do well to remember. But such production alterations tell only a part of the story. *Swan Lake* changes to some extent with every performance because, not only will each dancer attack the same steps in a distinctive way, but the same dancer will not execute the same steps in exactly the same way twice. With time the ballerina deepens her interpretation of a role, or becomes bored with it. Circumstances play their part as well; a new conductor in the pit, a new lover in the wings, each has an effect. And as the dancer's mood varies, so does her dancing.

Unlike a painting or a novel, a dance cannot be experienced directly as an intimate encounter between work and perceiver. When the work must be transmitted through an intermediary, through the person of a performer, then its material is constantly rethought, reshaped, reinterpreted. The audience comes to the dance through the agency of a personality who, no matter how hard he may try to be a merely colorless vessel through which the genius of the author is transmitted, somehow transmits a part of himself as well. Furthermore, the more closely he approaches the condition of the colorless vessel, the less interesting the dancer becomes as a performer.

But even if the original work could be preserved (as it can be now, on film) the audience itself has changed, bringing to it different stores of knowledge and experience and values. Even if the performers could reproduce exactly that first Maryinsky *Swan Lake*, the audience of the 1980s would not perceive it in the same manner as the audience of 1895. Most likely they would find the mime scenes boring and superfluous, for they are accustomed to a faster pace and to nondramatic dancing; few of the virtuoso feats would be impressive to eyes now familiar with pyrotechnics unknown to the inhabitants of tsarist Russia.

No single approach to the problem prevails. According to Frederick Ashton, a great ballet in time acquires a special patina that should not be tampered with. George Balanchine dissents, claiming that the ballet master who stages the revival should not feel constrained by the inconsistent memories of half-forgotten dances; he should try to conform to the spirit of Petipa rather than try literally to reconstruct an original that the choreographer himself undoubtedly altered from season to season.

In staging *Swan Lake*, most regisseurs seem to have sided with Balanchine rather than with Ashton, though to what extent they have conformed to the spirit of the original may well be questioned. A glance at even a few of the versions staged in the past half century reveals something of the tendencies. The plot line has been altered in a number of most divergent manners. Because officials of the Soviet Union disliked the moral tone of the tragic ending, Fyodor Lopukhov (1945) arranged a hand-to-hand combat in which Siegfried tore off Rothbart's wing, and a rosy glow filled the stage as Odette and Siegfried were united triumphantly. On the contrary, Erik Bruhn's production for the National Ballet of Canada (1966) had the prince destroyed at the end by the corps of swan maidens in a scene reminiscent of the demise of Orpheus. Still more critical, however, was Bruhn's casting Rothbart as a woman, a surrogate for the prince's domineering mother, who wants no rival for his affections (which provides a rather Freudian tint). Two years earlier, Rudolf Nureyev had produced a version in Vienna where the prince, a rather manic-depressive type, failed to win Odette and was killed by Rothbart. In Stuttgart (1963) John Cranko let Siegfried drown and left Odette waiting for the next prince. In the following decade, we find a production by the Scottish Ballet with choreography by Peter Darrell in which a group of Bad Companions display Odette to Siegfried. Benno then gives him a pipe, which induces the vision of scene 2, an idea borrowed from another Petipa ballet, *La Bayadère*. John Neumeier's version for the Hamburg Ballet (1976) had Ludwig of Bavaria as its central character. Confined, he recalled his past obsession with *Swan Lake* and identified himself with Siegfried, which accounted for scenes of "recollections."

Structural changes have been still more numerous, but I will mention just a few. Most obvious are the deletions which, at their extreme, condense the whole ballet to a single act (the St. Petersburg second). Balanchine's staging for the New York City Ballet consists of this act, but retains only the romantic adagio from Ivanov's choreography while adding a number of new ensemble numbers. In 1953 Vladimir Bourmeister of Moscow added a prologue showing the young princess innocently picking flowers when she is spied by Rothbart, and the audience sees him transform her into a swan. The Bolshoi Ballet added a jester in the third act and then put him into the first as well, the role gradually growing in importance as successive performers added their special flourishes. Nureyev composed a "yearning" solo for the prince at the end of the first act, an innovation that caught on and has been adopted for a number of productions. Some versions, by casting different ballerinas as Odette and Odile, allow for a real confrontation in the third act as the true swan queen tries to prevent Siegfried from being duped by her impersonator.

The full saga of the versions of *Swan Lake* produced by Britain's Royal Ballet would take more space than can be allowed here, but the major contributions of Frederick Ashton may be noted. They include, in 1952, a valse pas de six in act 1 and the Neapolitan Dance in act 3; in 1963, a prologue (dropped in 1967), a new pas de six and a pas de quatre in act 1 (the latter was eventually moved to act 3, allowing for the reinstatement of the Petipa pas de trois in act 1), a Spanish dance in act 3, and completely new choreography for the last act (later abandoned when the Ivanov version was revived).

One specific step deserves attention, since we will have to return to it later because it exemplifies a number of problems. This is the set of brilliant pirouettes, the thirty-two fouettés with which Odile dazzles Siegfried in act 3. They are often regarded as a much-anticipated tour de force—sacrosanct, some would say. Yet historical considerations might weaken the arguments that try to claim that they are necessary. There seems no reason to doubt that their original inclusion was due simply to the casting of Legnani in the leading role of *Swan Lake*. A brilliant technician, Legnani was—in 1895—the only woman in the world who could do those thirty-two whipped pirouettes on pointe, and her audience expected to see the feat whenever they saw her. Even Petipa dared not omit them, though he certainly arranged a most opportune moment for their performance. Whether the audience appreciated their dramatic appropriateness may be doubted, for it was said that the balletomanes counted the turns aloud, bursting into wild applause at their successful conclusion. Why not follow Petipa in spirit and let the star of the moment execute her own specialité de la maison, whatever it happens to be? Thus, Maya Plisetskaya has substituted a rapid circle of piqué tours around the stage. Some viewers find this disappointing, although they do not go so far as to claim that the change has violated the identity of *Swan Lake*.

If plot and characters can be so radically altered, if dances can be shifted from one place to another, added or omitted, how can we identify *Swan Lake*?

The ballet has not survived in its pristine state, but it has survived; some continuing strain of recognizable identity has been preserved. Though we may see many variant interpretations, we seem to perceive an essential core that is *Swan Lake*. That is, we frequently perceive it, for on occasion we are uncomfortably aware that something has gone awry and *Swan Lake* is no longer there. What is this essence that we find or miss?

The most cogent approach to this question that I have encountered is that of Mikel Dufrenne, who asks, "Can we not say that the performance always invents, so to speak, the truth of the work? . . . Its truth is not fixed beforehand and several interpretations of the same work are possible, with the result that it changes meaning with the times." To Dufrenne, a great work is inexhaustible, for its significance can be endlessly renewed as successive performers endow it with fresh insights, each time disclosing further facets of its meaning. *Swan Lake* may be seen with validity from a number of points of view; it may be presented as a simple, humanly touching love story or as a majestic declaration on the nature of good and evil. One era will conceive it as romance, another as melodrama, and still another will interpret it as classical tragedy. But we never perceive it without interpretation. We come in contact with the truth of the work—or rather the truths of the work—only through its performances; they alone complete it, reveal it to us. Yet for Dufrenne there is also a reality of the work that exists apart from its performances, a reality that makes demands on those performances. In relation to this reality, we find a performance either revealing a fresh truth about the work or playing it false.

Most of us usually do delight in seeing a great work over and over again, because we enjoy the fresh nuances revealed by a new performer, because we discover new meanings in familiar motions that are given an unfamiliar accent. But sometimes we are not delighted; we wince with displeasure to see an aspect of performance or production that appears not merely weak but downright wrong. We feel that the work itself—not just our personal image of it, which is another matter—has been betrayed. The reality of the work has not been respected. Dufrenne asserts that we discover this through perceiving a lack of harmony in the performance. A good rendition, he notes, seems to fade away in the presence of the work, while a poor one distracts us from the work by calling attention to itself. For dance, he could have cited the star who always appears as himself regardless of the nature of the character he is supposedly playing.

We might also consider the intrusion of inappropriate qualities—a disturbing dynamic or tempo, an overly (or insufficiently) elaborate decor—which can break the spell. But how does the audience identify this spell? Dufrenne calls it "a certain atmosphere in which subject, music, and choreography cooperate and which forms the soul of the ballet." This, however, may be deceiving, for a director may create a perfectly harmonious ambience in which all the elements fully complement and enhance one another, yet the resulting atmosphere is quite different from that of previous productions. Something more than internal consistency is involved. Can we be more specific about the identity of that atmosphere?

Nelson Goodman suggests a path of investigation when he distinguishes between the constitutive and the contingent properties of a performance work. Some matters, the constitutive, are strictly prescribed for a proper realization while others, the contingent, are optional. Compliance is necessary only in the case of the former, which any enactment must possess in order to qualify as a performance of this particular work. Unlike Dufrenne, Goodman attaches no distinct aesthetic value to his criterion; the standard he describes is purely numerical, since compliance can be simply checked by reference to a text or notated score. However, his distinction between constitutive and contingent properties might be viewed in relation not only to the factual correspondence between score and performance but to the manner in which the artist succeeds or fails in using his options to reveal a genuine truth of the work. To apply this concept we must first try to determine which properties in a dance could be considered constitutive and which could be considered the domain of interpretation.

Are individual steps constitutive? Looking back at experiences of *Swan Lake*, we soon realize that we have seen steps changed when it did not matter and we have seen them changed when it did matter. Discussing the work of Balanchine, Suzanne Farrell remarked that his choreography "does not reside in the steps. The choreography is in the process and the structure. The steps just show it. The steps can be anything . . . [but] he knows what he wants in terms of order, structure, how and when things are going to happen." Ashton, too, did not refer to particular steps when he described his admiration for *Sleeping Beauty*: "A miracle of choreographic construction, forms, and brilliantly thought-out climaxes."

This, however, is not at all the way Antony Tudor's dancers talk about his choreography. In his dramatic works, Tudor conceived of character in terms of physical images. Hugh Laing has described the "key movements" in *Pillar of Fire*: "for the Younger Sister, a toss of the head; for Hagar, pulling at her collar; for the Elder Sister, putting on her gloves . . . for the Young Man, a sharp thrust with one leg." If a change is made in a key movement, the characterization is altered, even lost. Apparently the reconstruction of a Tudor ballet has to proceed strictly, with minute attention to detail; for example, the head is not simply inclined, it must be tossed, indicating a casual willfulness. Balanchine is seldom concerned with characterization, but he is concerned with structure, which means that the steps cannot quite be "anything." They must fall within a category of compliance, they must fit his idea of process and structure for a particular ballet. The jagged thrusts of *Agon* would be inappropriate to the flowing lyricism of *Serenade*. Although any step can be altered in terms of such variables as how energy is applied to it and when it occurs within a phrase, there are limits. A leap cannot be sustained indefinitely in time; some movements must be done in one spot while others have to travel in space. Balanchine chooses from a finite range of possibilities. Still his range is broader than Tudor's because his needs are more generalized. Different kinds of dances should not be expected to have the same kind of constituent properties.

Where does the director of a new production of *Swan Lake* turn for guidance? Petipa left no useful directions. If only there had been a film of the first performance! But as Dufrenne noted, any performance reveals only one of a great work's potentially inexhaustible store of truths; if we insisted that later performances comply with all the properties of the first, we would place an unfair restriction on them, and on ourselves as audience as well.

How about a notated score? Of which version of the work?

The first one? Or the one that the choreographer said he considered best (though both the audience and the critics panned it)? I doubt that any creative artist in another field can rival the choreographer in the number of successive alterations made to a work. It was once said that Balanchine changed a woman's variation whenever he became fascinated by another length of leg. Should the score include all his alternatives? How about the one actually devised in a moment of inspiration by ballerina number six—the one the choreographer called his own favorite version? We are left with the question of identity. Which version is the Work?

So next week you are going to see *Swan Lake*. Some facets of your experience may be predicted. You are definitely not going to see the choreography of either the Reisinger or the Petipa-Ivanov *Swan Lake* as it was done originally. Or even the latter as it was produced by the Diaghilev Ballet Russe in 1911 or by the Vic-Wells Ballet in 1934 or by the New York City Ballet in 1951 or by the National Ballet of Canada in 1966 or by the American Ballet Theatre in 1967. You may, however, see some parts of several of these. You will not see Odette/Odile exactly as she was conceived by Legnani or by such successors as Galina Ulanova or Margot Fonteyn, though the ballerina you do see may well incorporate some aspects of those earlier interpretations into her own. You may or may not see Benno. You will probably not hear all of Tchaikovsky's original score, and you may likely hear some music that Tchaikovsky did not write. You will undoubtedly see some period costumes, though of what period is uncertain. You may leave the theatre saddened by the tragic ending or gladdened by the death of the evil Rothbart and the union of the virtuous lovers. You may see a true *Swan Lake*.

Through all this can we discern the real *Swan Lake*?

Before this question can be answered we have to investigate a number of others. It is easy enough to say that we are looking for the constitutive properties of a particular ballet, but numerous arguments and counterarguments have been advanced with regard to what properties a dance work of any kind needs to possess. Some early answers relating to theatrical forms focused on plot and character, often with the additional stipulation of a valid moral point, but few such proposals have been made for some time. "Let us dance and sing, then," cried Clive Bell in the early years of this century, "for singing and dancing are true arts, useless materially, valuable only for their aesthetic significance. Above all, let us dance and devise dances—dancing is a very pure art, a creation of abstract form."

Naturally, ideas of what is essential to a dance will vary, depending on one's concept of its purpose. In the next chapter we will review some of the ideas people have held about the function of dance. We will then see that all have agreed—in general—that the medium of dance is human movement. But what kind of human movement? Dance is not the cheerleaders marching in a parade or the adroit maneuvers of the tennis player. Or is it? The answer requires a defense, defining the properties that are shared and those that are exclusive to one activity and not to the other. Does dance movement have to communicate some significance beyond the facts of its direction in space and duration in time? On the other hand, is it possible that the nature of the movement alone is not sufficient to justify the title of "dance"?

If we are to identify *Swan Lake* as a particular kind of dance, we should be able to do so by describing its manner of dealing with the elements essential to theatrical dance. From there we can seek the constitutive properties that make *Swan Lake* the particular ballet that it is. And the contingent properties that make it a repository for ever-new truths.

Pierina Legnani was Odette in 1895. *From Yury Slonimsky,* "Writings on Lev Ivanov."

Legnani's softly raised arm set a model of gentleness observed by Lupe Serrano, seen here with Enrique Martinez as Benno and Royes Fernandez as Siegfried in the American Ballet Theatre production of 1958. *Photo by Fred Fehl.*

Alexis D. Boulgakov was Rothbart, the evil magician, in 1895. *From Slonimsky, "Writings."*

Celia Franca was both the queen mother and the magician to Erik Bruhn's Siegfried in 1967. *Photo by Fred Fehl.*

"No, you can't be Benno, the Prince's Friend; he doesn't exist anymore."

Drawing by Edward Gorey. From The Lavender Leotard.

2. Actions and Passions, Airs and Graces

Auguste Vestris, seen in an English caricature of 1781, was known for his technical prowess. However, someone is said to have remarked of his feats: "Any goose can do as much." What is dance? Is it difficult movement or beautiful movement? Or something else again?

ANTHROPOLOGIST Adrienne Kaeppler has defined dance as "a cultural form that results from creative processes which manipulate human bodies in time and space." She continues with a warning: "Every society has its own way of thinking about its cultural forms and what is aesthetically relevant for one society will not necessarily be aesthetically relevant for another." To illustrate she cites three cultural forms of Japan: *mikagura*, performed in Shinto shrines, *buyo*, performed in Kabuki drama, and *bon*, performed to honor the dead. Westerners would consider these three kinds of dance, but to the Japanese they are simply the movement dimension of three entirely different activities that function in three entirely distinct ways within the society to which they belong.

Even within the western tradition dance serves a number of distinct functions: to confuse the values of ritual dance with those of recreational dance or of theatrical dance results only in distortion. Though aesthetic values may be found in all of them, these values are essential only to the last, and their absence from religious or social dancing in no way lowers the capacity of those forms to function in manners perfectly appropriate to the ends they are intended to serve.

The western world has, on occasion, deemed dance a "sublime activity—a kind of kinetic analogy for the divine order." On other occasions, however, this same segment of the globe has chosen to consider dance "a grotesque spectacle," fit only for contempt and ridicule. Havelock Ellis called it "the loftiest, the most moving, the most beautiful of the arts." But Sir Joshua Reynolds likened dancing masters to hairdressers and tailors, claiming that all three distort and disfigure the human form. Over the years dance has been blamed for corrupting the morals of youth and for the disintegration of kingdoms. Yet it has been praised for its values in the areas of health, recreation, courtship, and entertainment.

The status of dance within a culture has often been influenced by the position accorded it in relation to the other arts. Paul Oskar Kristeller noted that the ancients generally linked dance and music as elements of poetry; this balance was altered by the Pythagorean discovery of the numerical proportions underlying musical intervals, after which music was likened to mathematics and opposed to poetry and dance. The Middle Ages made a point of separating the liberal from the mechanical arts (the latter including agriculture, medicine, and theatre), but by the seventeenth century the division most often referred to was that between the arts and the sciences, with music sometimes in one camp, sometimes in the other, and dance rather lost between the two. In 1710 Abbé Massieu defined three categories of arts: those that polish the spirit (eloquence, poetry, history, and grammar), those that aim for diversion and honest pleasure (painting, sculpture, music, and dance), and those that serve the necessities of life (agriculture, navigation, and architecture). In 1746 the influential Abbé Batteux separated the mechanical arts from the fine arts, the latter having pleasure as their end and including music, poetry, painting, sculpture, and dance. Regrettably for us, however, dance did not maintain its eighteenth-century status, for Kristeller, writing in 1952, summarized the current attitude, which defined five "major" arts as fundamental to the modern system; on these five, he asserted, "all writers and thinkers seem to agree." They were painting, sculpture, architecture, music, and poetry. Some other arts, Kristeller admitted, were occasionally added, depending on "the different views and interests of the authors." He listed these as follows: "gardening, engraving and the decorative arts, the dance and the theatre, sometimes the opera, and finally eloquence and prose literature."

The place of dance in these hierarchies naturally reflects the prevailing value system of the society, but with a peculiar qualification. Western civilization has long been characterized by a compulsion to exalt the spirit over the flesh, the mind over the body. Though Americans tend to blame our Puritan forebears for this situation, the attitude may be found throughout the Judeo-Christian tradition. Because of its physicality, dance was often treated as a lesser art, its values considered minor manifestations of qualities better exhibited by some other, more spiritual medium. Still, over the centuries, the art found many defenders.

In Greece, Plato abolished dance—along with all the other arts—from the ideal republic, whose citizens were capable of pure thought and had no need of sensory images. In Book 7 of the *Laws*, though, Plato was concerned with a more practical social structure, and here he admitted two forms of the art of Terpsichore: gymnastic, which was an aid to health and beauty, and theatrical dance. The function of the latter was similar to the function of music. Both served to preserve the dignity and freedom of the citizen, reflecting the harmony of a noble and ordered mind; their virtues were simplicity, measure, and symmetry. Aristotle preferred to stress the closeness to drama: "even the dancer [like the actor] imitates men's characters as well as what they do and suffer." The analogies to music and drama would be used for centuries thereafter.

In the second century A.D., Lucian of Samosata referred to the dance of the planets as they turn, each in its proper sphere, as an instance of cosmic choreography. A similar Pythagorean concern with the orderly arrangement of numbers reappears in Balthazar de Beaujoyeulx's 1581 concept of a ballet as "no more than the geometrical grouping of people dancing together, accompanied by the varied harmony of several instruments." The libretto for his *Ballet Comique de la Reine* describes numerical designs: twelve pages enter, six from one side and six from the other; then twelve nymphs similarly; the dancers then form a triangle and subsequently arrange themselves in circles and squares. Some ten years later, in England, Sir John Davies called dance an imitation of the harmony of nature, a "moving all in measure" like the "movings of the heavens" with "comely order and proportion fair." In

France, in 1682, Claude Menestrier remarked that Pythagoras had considered God to be a number and a harmony and therefore argued that man should honor him with measured cadence.

But even as Menestrier wrote, faith in that cosmic order was waning. Fortunately, the author was able to supply an alternative source of significance for the art. Dance, he admitted, exhibited patterns of numerical order, but a ballet—the most perfect form of dance—could express both the actions and the sentiments of men; it was truly, as Aristotle had asserted, an imitative art, though what it really imitated was not the orderly movement of the cosmos but the much more unruly movements of the men who inhabit the earth. Further, dance was unique among the arts in its power to depict the passions, using, for example, tender gestures to express love, violent ones to show anger. However, Menestrier did not trust movement alone to convey the message, for he frequently commented on the importance of verses, costumes, and machines to clarify the various characters and situations of the ballet.

Theories promoting the dramatic qualities of dance proliferated in the eighteenth century, with increasing emphasis on the dancer's body as the chief medium of expression. Theatrical dance had made tremendous technical strides since the time of Menestrier, but in 1712 John Weaver lamented that his contemporaries were using their new skills only to represent "modulated motion," whereas they were capable of realizing the true function of stage dancing, which was imitation, "to explain Things conceiv'd in the Mind, by the Gestures and Motions of the Body, and plainly and intelligibly representing Actions, Manners, and Passions." Sadly he remarked that most audiences preferred the capering and tumbling of modulated motion to productions that fulfilled the dramatic purpose of theatre dance, thus defining a duality of values that has continued to occupy dance thinkers to our own day.

What is the proper function of dance? To entertain and amaze with feats of virtuosity? Then how does it differ from the circus?

To move the emotions with scenes of pity and terror? Then how does it differ from drama? And these extremes only begin to establish the problems opened up by the eighteenth-century thinkers. Weaver distinguished the "Excellency of the Art," its imitative qualities, from the "Beauties," its formal patterns. What about movement that is simply beautiful to watch or pleasing in its subtle musicality? Are there limits to the kinds of actions that the dancer can, or should, represent? What about genres? While the eighteenth-century dancers concentrated on improving their technique, the theorists pondered questions of essence and value.

Of major concern for the time was the ballet d'action. All agreed that these narrative dances were depictions of nature, but most often the idea was limited to the pleasant aspects of nature. *"La belle nature!"* cried the French, urging the faithful portrayal of a beautiful world. A ballet, declared Jean Georges Noverre in 1760, is nature itself, but nature "embellished with every ornament of the art." He urged the choreographer to be selective, to avoid tedious episodes that might hold up the action, leaving insufficient time for the display of delightful tableaux and groupings. By the dawn of the nineteenth century, selectivity had turned into the idealization that culminated in the great ballets of the romantic period, with their exotic settings and winged sylphs. "After all," claimed Théophile Gautier in 1837, "dancing consists of nothing more than the art of displaying beautiful shapes in graceful positions and the development from them of lines agreeable to the eye; it is mute rhythm, music that is seen. Dancing is little adapted to render metaphysical themes; it only expresses the passions; love, desire with all its attendant coquetry." But while technical accomplishments multiplied, the fashion for sylphs waned. Beauty, noted Mikhail Fokine in 1916, had lost out to acrobatics.

What is beautiful? To Isadora Duncan, Fokine's balletic movements were ugly. He called them idealized. Both believed that dance should be expressive, while their contemporary André Levinson felt that all advocates of dramatic ballet had confused the values of dance with those of pantomime. The proper approach, he argued, was to look for those characteristics that belong exclusively to this art, to the "intrinsic beauty of a dance step . . . its esthetic reason for being," since the aim of dance is to "create beauty." In the 1940s, however, Martha Graham did not speak of dancing beautifully; she wanted to dance significantly, to portray the "interior landscape," which might not be "beautiful" in the conventional sense, though it would be undeniably meaningful. Could choreographers ever consider dispensing with both beauty and meaning? They could and did. Lucinda Childs described her *Untitled Solo* of 1968: "A continuum of simple movements . . . such as kneeling, sitting, lying on the back, rolling, squatting, lunging forward onto one leg or jumping. . . . There were set variations in speeds and distances covered while executing the movements, and the dance ended when the possibilities for the combinations of variables were exhausted."

What, then, is dance? Imitation of actions and passions, according to Weaver in 1712. Not at all, retorted Adam Smith before the century had ended: "Every Dance is in reality a succession of airs and graces." And so the controversy has continued, though not without complications regarding the nature of the actions and passions appropriate to portrayal in dance or regarding the definition of what constitute pleasing airs and graces. Is the true function of dance to give delight or to stir the emotions? A ballet, wrote an anonymous critic in 1848, is "a good excuse for a three-day lunacy," admitting that his glimpse of a ballerina soaring through the air made him want to leave the soles of his boots. On seeing Martha Graham in 1929 John Martin commented, "She does the unforgivable thing for a dancer to do . . . she makes you think. . . .She leaves you upheaved and disquieted and furnishes after-thoughts not calculated to soothe such a condition."

The gamut could hardly be broader. Yet the subject of all these writers was dance, and we have limited the area surveyed to Europe and America, starting only with the Greeks and skipping numerous interesting byways. Disagreement has been rife on al-most every topic—the function of dance, the range and pertinence of its representational capacities, the nature of the effect it can or should have on its audience. One factor has not been questioned: that the medium of dance is human movement. To be sure, the exclusivity of that medium has been challenged, for choreogra-phers through the ages have relied on a variety of other moving objects to enhance their effects. Elaborate machines, which carried performers on and off the playing area, were prominent in the French ballet de cour and the English masque of the Renaissance. "Transformation scenes"—such as a garden suddenly turned into a palace—were attractive features of nineteenth-century ballets. Music, decor, costumes, lighting—all have been utilized. Yet de-spite their often substantial contribution to the total effect, these have never been called essential to the nature of the art. The fundamental element is human movement; without this, we may have theatre—but we cannot have dance. Further, we find quite general assent to the idea that there is something distinctive about the kind of movement we call dance. Whether there is agreement about the nature of that distinction is another matter.

Aristotle specified the rhythms of the dancer's attitudes, and rhythm turns out to be a property that is frequently attributed to dance movement. In the eighteenth century, Denis Diderot's en-cyclopedia cited movement that is ordered and measured; in the twentieth, Thomas Munro specified "rhythmical bodily move-ment presenting an ordered sequence of moving visual patterns." "Regulated" also recurs in definitions. Clearly, the movement most generally considered dance is movement that has been sub-jected to some kind of forming process. Consequently, attempts to define the nature of dance movement often begin by drawing a distinction between dance and "ordinary" movement.

Of the various treatments of this issue, one of the most inter-esting is that of Paul Valéry. He begins by locating dance among those human movements that can be consciously willed, as opposed to those that are involuntary; he then separates those conscious movements that have an exterior aim, and that consequently end when that aim has been accomplished, from those not so related to an object beyond themselves, and that therefore do not end with the completion of a task. These two types of movement are further differentiated in relation to the law of economy of effort, which is essential to the first kind and essentially irrelevant to the second. Movement of the latter sort need not follow any particular path in space; it may even be quite chaotic, as it is in children's play. But there is one manifestation of such movement that is highly ordered, though its order is not determined by any practical function. This is the state of dancing, which seems to engender a special kind of exhilaration, evoking within us the idea of a transcendent sphere of existence. The dancer seems to belong to a constellation other than our own where she breathes unbounded energy. There she exists at ease, a pure essence of music and movement. She makes our ordinary acts, tailored to serve our commonplace needs, appear coarse against her vibrancy, against her exaltation.

Dance movement, then, is voluntary. Animals "dance" only metaphorically because their actions are programmed by their biological structures. Inanimate objects also "dance" only by analogy. "Pink Rocker" rolls forward and backward, right on the beat of its musical accompaniment, then jiggles itself about in a circle till it finally exits offstage, having allowed Betty Jones and Fritz Lüdin time to change their costumes. A "dance"? No. But a fitting, entertaining interlude in a dance concert. True dance movement is willed.

Most analysts would agree with Valéry that dance movement is not practical; it is not executed for the purpose of attaining a goal that exists apart from the movement itself. Gautier eliminated useful things from the category of the beautiful, of course including dance among things beautiful. More specifically, Edwin Denby comments that dance steps "don't give the body that useful patient look that walking does." Some of the criteria of practical movement seem to be quite irrelevant when applied to dance. In everyday living where tasks are to be accomplished, economy of movement is desirable; the idea is to move only as much as is necessary in order to do the job. Dance is similar, in that it strives to avoid unnecessary movement—those extra heaves and jerks that serve only to betray the expenditure of effort. But viewed from a practical standpoint, dance movement often takes the long way around, deliberately making motions that—while delightful to watch—contribute nothing toward getting from one place to another as directly as possible.

Erwin Straus notes that dance, unlike ordinary movement, involves the use of the trunk, a part of the body usually kept rigidly vertical. Asking about the effect produced by the dancer's departures from the vertical plane, Straus finds that "all these trunk movements—the turning and bowing, lowering and raising, inclining and rocking—are not particularly functional for advancing in a straight line. They do not help to keep the body in one direction, but rather they force it out of a straight line." The straight line is usually the most practical path between two points. Much less useful is the meandering course that William Hogarth called the line of beauty, the serpentine, which he found most beautifully in the minuet.

Recently Monroe Beardsley suggested that dance has "more zest, vigor, fluency, expansiveness, or stateliness than appears necessary for its practical purposes, there is an overflow or superfluity of expressiveness to mark it as belonging to the domain of dance." Practical expressiveness is something we see constantly in everyday life; the hand shoots across in warning or reaches out in welcome. But dance expressiveness is something else again. Beardsley described it as extravagant. The reason is easily seen in Lincoln Kirstein's apt phrase about the need for making movement "theatrically legible." The dancer has to project his feeling from a performing area to an audience seated somewhere beyond that area. To communicate in a theatrical situation, the choreographer alters natural movement until it assumes a shape that may well be extravagant in relation to its original purpose. Such speed, such strength, such extension in space are not necessary to accomplish the task or communicate the message. But the ordinary shape of the movement is too familiar to command attention for its own sake. Stylization, which exaggerates its features, captures the interest of the audience.

Ideas of what constitutes dance movement, what distinguishes it from the actions of everyday life, have changed with time. The nature of efficient movement has not changed, because biologically the human animal remains basically the same. Like social values, however, artistic values have varied; movement at one time considered elegant is at another deemed artificial, and what was delightfully spontaneous to one generation is seen as sloppy by the next. Dance styles embody qualities that pleased their original audiences but may bore and even antagonize some—though perhaps not all—succeeding ones. Under the circumstances, it is somewhat surprising that we accept so many nineteenth-century ballet conventions, which include the use of a technique that began to take form in the courts of Renaissance Europe and that reflected the aesthetic, social, and ethical values of those courts, which were very different from the values of present-day America. The technique, it seems, turned out to be marvelously adaptable, surviving a series of apparently antithetical visual and dramatic contexts and even managing to coexist with styles of most divergent orders.

The nature of the basic stylization of movement in classical ballet may be likened to the eighteenth-century concept of poetic diction, which involved a studied avoidance of common manners of speech that would offend the fastidious taste of the sensitive reader, and a complementary concern with refinement. Ballet technique developed in the elegant ambience of the eighteenth-century balls and royal theatres. It began with social dancing. If a French princess enjoyed watching the dances of the peasants, she would nevertheless learn their steps only after her dancing master had adapted them to accommodate the limited range of movement permitted by her heeled slippers and her tightly laced corset. Thus, the stately minuet was descended from the sprightly, rural branle de Poitou; the hearty, swinging steps of the folk were transformed into dainty, mincing pas. When the ballet master took over, further changes were made: flexed feet became pointed, shorter skirts allowed a slight extension of the leg. As the minuet moved onto the proscenium stage, its intricate serpentine floor patterns became less significant; soloists appeared, soon learning that they could easily insert an extra turn, a more elaborate jump, with no objection from the authorities and with much applause from the audience. A display of uncommon skill, providing it entailed no loss of dignity, was considered perfectly appropriate to the characters of the gods and epic heroes who then dominated the ballet stage.

In his 1800 preface to the *Lyrical Ballads*, Wordsworth contended that the language of "humble and rustic life" was to be preferred by the poet, because the men who spoke it were closer to "the beautiful and permanent forms of nature." English poetry was profoundly affected by his ideas, but the language of ballet remained, for the time being, untouched. On the contrary, thanks to its growing professionalism, the dance vocabulary became increasingly skilled, increasingly removed from the actions of ordinary life. By the early nineteenth century, Noverre's demand for the depiction of beautiful nature had been submerged in the delights of technical accomplishment. Why bother with portrayals of character and emotion when the audience was just waiting to applaud the next trick? With the adoption of romantic themes, replete with ethereal sylphs and wilis, the new accomplishments—higher leaps and especially pointe work—found dramatic justification. The themes of romanticism called for a new mode of stylization—less rigid, lighter, more flowing. The sylph was a child of nature, innocent, unspoiled, and therefore exempt from the rules of both courtly decorum and epic grandeur. But as the woodland sprites and their ever-yearning lovers gradually waned in public enthusiasm, ballet was left with its technique—polished and spectacular. Petipa used it with heightened elegance, with coolly symmetrical designs framing sequences of brilliant technical display. Vera Krasovskaya has suggested that his *Sleeping Beauty* is closer in form to symphony than to drama: "It is precisely the maximum coincidence of musical and choreographic high points that determines the artistic perfection of the production." A co-incidence of narrative and choreographic high points would denote a very different kind of production.

To Fokine, at the turn of the twentieth century, the absence of dramatic reference had made ballet "acrobatic, mechanical, and empty." Like Wordsworth, he proposed a return to "the beautiful and permanent forms of nature." For dance, this meant defining the principles of natural movements. Fokine sought to find them in those gestures that appear to be indicators of feeling and to heighten those gestures into "the development and ideal of the sign." This went beyond practical expressiveness because the movement was "developed," intensified, so that its meaning was not only clear but capable of stirring the emotions of the audience. It was "idealized" so that it not only communicated but also pleased with its sensuous beauty. For Fokine dance movement was "based on the laws of natural expression," but he made no pretense of using "natural" in the sense of "ordinary."

Nor did his admired contemporary Duncan, who, in advocating movement in harmony with the forms of nature, took as her models the waves of the sea and the branches of trees swayed by the wind. People would move as beautifully as these, she claimed, if society had not spoiled them with the restrictive clothing and artificial manners that made ordinary movement so ugly. For both choreographers, the search for what was more "natural" led to a selection and modification of common movements, producing a special theatrical vocabulary, one that was appropriate to the character and situation represented in the case of Fokine, and to the emotion expressed in the case of Duncan.

Other rebels appeared, each seeing the need for a new formulation of the language of dance. As Owen Barfield claimed for a similar stage in the evolution of poetry, the old modes had become familiar; they had lost their power to move an audience to fresh, meaningful insights. The rebels sought to revitalize the language by stripping it of outmoded stylization. Ruth St. Denis chose to adopt the stylizations of other cultures—of Egypt, India, Japan—because they seemed closer to her concept of mystic reality than those of her own culture. Martha Graham referred to the need "to make apparent once again the inner hidden realities behind the accepted symbols." But for Graham, as for Mary Wigman and Doris Humphrey, no existing idiom was adequate. Rejecting St. Denis's self-conscious adaptation of exoticism, they looked for movement that would be more compelling than Duncan's simple lyricism but devoid of the affected elegance that they associated with the ballet. They strove to find more basic roots—roots they shared with the "common man." Graham choreographed "Revolt" and "Immigrant"; Humphrey made "Speed" and "Descent into a Dangerous Place." For new themes they had to invent a new movement vocabulary relevant to their own time and place, a world forever changed by the psychoanalytical concepts of Freud, by the cubism of Picasso, and the atonality of Schönberg. They needed a new way to call attention through movement to this new way of looking at the world. Unfortunately, most of the general public found that reality distasteful; they still wanted flowing waltzes on tiptoe—beautiful nature. Instead, the early modern dance gave them tense, angular, percussive movements that exposed the often brutal facets of nature.

By midcentury, however, new influences came to bear on the forms of dance stylization. Feeling that there was much in nature that man did not understand, Merce Cunningham and his colleagues, noted Carolyn Brown, "chose to open themselves and their works to the possible influences beyond their conscious knowledge. This was an act of affirmation, they felt, an entering into the totality of existence. The creator (artist) assumes a more humble place in the natural scheme of things than the role of the self made 'genius'." Cunningham relied on certain chance procedures to put his movement in touch with nature. Although he dispensed with deliberate, formal organization, Cunningham continued to use stylized movement, much of it deriving from the fundamental tenets of classicism. This skilled vocabulary became the target of the 1960s avant-garde who wished to throw out every vestige of what was traditionally considered "dance" movement. Yvonne Rainer explored the alternatives: "stand, walk, run, eat, carry bricks, show movies." The members of the Judson Dance Theatre, founders of what has become known as "postmodern" dance, resolved to choreograph with "ordinary" movement and untrained "dancers." If dance is human movement that has been intensified or idealized in any of the manners we have just described, then these performers could not be said to "dance."

This time, however, other criteria were being invoked. Roman Jakobson has stated the structuralist position: "In poetry any verbal element is converted into a figure of poetic speech." From this point of view no movement in and by itself is independently distinguishable as dance apart from its role in a system of relationships that give substance to otherwise insignificant materials. If the Judson choreographers did not alter the configuration of ordinary movements, they nevertheless presented them in a situation that separated audience from performers and consequently focused the attention of the viewer in an extraordinary way. For the dancers, their everyday actions served no everyday functions; their walks and crawls and limp encounters served to display the natural motions of the body going about its daily tasks as an object of inherent interest. The movement was considered worth perceiving for its own sake quite apart from its task function, which merely provided a device of organization. This would satisfy

Valéry's stipulation that dance movement is not directed to practical ends, though it would contradict most previous views that sought to eliminate from the province of dance the bare, useful look of movement that was not heightened through stylization. For the Judson choreographers and their followers, the context that framed their activity provided stylization enough to make the movement perceivable as dance, to transform it into an aesthetic object. The audience did not always agree.

Through all these developments ballet technique survived, incorporating greater use of the middle body and a wider range of dynamic qualities after the advent of the expressive modern dance, but becoming more virtuosic when the adherents of postmodern dance championed the use of everyday motion. Still choreographers such as Ashton and Balanchine pursued their individual courses, subtly manipulating and extending the technique to serve their personal stylistic needs. The distance between 1890s classical and 1980s neoclassical ballet is considerable. Audiences now accustomed to the Balanchine version of *Swan Lake* might well find Ivanov's lake scene static and full of irrelevant, nondance gesture, whereas St. Petersburg might have considered the New York City Ballet approach overly energetic and lacking in poetic atmosphere. The answer with regard to the exact place of dance in relation to ordinary movement, pantomime, and acrobatics may depend on when and where and how the question is asked.

Perhaps dance is what it is when and where it happens, and we only distort matters when we try to reduce it to a single, unchangeable entity; this has long been the argument of the ethnologists. We may recall Adrienne Kaeppler's warning that "what is aesthetically relevant for one society will not necessarily be aesthetically relevant for another." But problems occur within a society as well. Sometimes inappropriate preconceptions, derived from necessarily limited personal experience, get in the way, making it difficult if not impossible for the spectator to relate to the event as a performance of dance. In certain cases, information beyond what the senses can discern is required, and it is the recognition of this need that has caused some recent conceptual artists to provide extensive explanatory program notes for their concerts. Arthur Danto suggests that here it is theory that makes the work a member of the world of art, and when a choreographer stretches that theory beyond the level already familiar to his audience, he risks misunderstanding and even the verdict that what he has created is not "art."

The problems of an avant-garde are well known; less obvious are the problems of tradition. *Swan Lake* has been so frequently updated because succeeding generations have lost touch with certain aspects of the artworld that gave significance to particular aspects of the original production. The rather arbitrary gestures that designated such messages as "the lake is full of my mother's tears" belonged to an accepted convention that today's audience would find dull and uninformative. The Maryinsky felt no need to provide dramatic motivation for Odile's fouettés, but some modern versions have brought Siegfried on stage to admire them, thus accelerating the emotional climax. Would a full understanding of the Petipa/Ivanov artworld enable us to appreciate *Swan Lake* in its original form?

What did dance mean to Russia in 1895? The world then knew nothing of postmodern or even of modern dance; Isadora Duncan had not yet come along. The company of dancers at the Maryinsky Theatre was trained in a school that adhered rigidly to the five turned-out positions of the legs, an erect torso, rounded arms. (Not much later Fokine complained that if he asked a dancer simply to run naturally, she did not know what do do.) Years of systematic training went into molding the balletic body, disciplined by the refined training techniques of the French and only recently strengthened by the more vigorous practice of the Italians. Along with their purely classical training, the dancers were taught a number of "character" dances, folk forms considerably removed from their earthy originals, but nevertheless comparatively unrestrained in style. Traditional mime was also included in the dancer's education. Advanced students learned excerpts from the repertory, either from the dancers who had created the roles or from their immediate successors. At times respect for old glories amounted to reverence.

The school faculty guarded tradition and so did the audience of the Maryinsky Theatre. The entourage of the tsar, various orders of dignitaries and their families, officers, foreign ambassadors, and members of aristocratic societies made up the large subscription audience, which zealously held on to the most desirable of the twenty-five hundred seats in the elegant blue, cream, and gold theatre. Tamara Karsavina described them: "knowledgeable, exacting . . . conservative in the extreme. A new venture, the slightest variation from the old canons was heresy to them." Their concerns, however, were limited: a favorite dancer, an admired variation, must be safeguarded. But a ballet as a whole was considered rather as a collection of miscellaneous, largely independent items. A dull scene could be dropped without complaint if a popular pas de deux (perhaps from another work altogether) were inserted in its place. If a ballerina had a preferred variation or one for which she was well known, the audience expected her to perform it, regardless of the role she was playing.

The critics did not attend the premiere of *Swan Lake* expecting to find either an artistic masterpiece or a wildly exciting, innovative experiment. The latter, of course, would never have passed the censors. The former actually happened, but was—predictably—ignored. Apart from their indifference to Tchaikovsky's magnificent score, the critics commented primarily, not on the choreography, but on the dancing. The reviewer in *Novoe Vremya* remarked of Legnani: "For her, it seems there is no such thing as difficulty. To grace, artistry, precision, and confidence, she joins the extraordinary strength of the steel muscles of her beautifully shaped legs." The critic for *Novosti* singled out the now-famous pas de deux in the second scene but did not credit its beauty to

Ivanov: "The adagio is a *chef d'oeuvre* in the execution of the ballerina; she revealed in it a brilliant technique, lightness of movement and plastique of poses." The plot apparently mattered not at all, though the *Russkaya Musikalnaya Gazeta* did lament the lack of an aura of fantasy, which the writer considered necessary to produce the atmosphere of the poetic old tale. The dramatic expressiveness of the dancing was not noted at all. Perhaps it did not exist, but if so, its absence was apparently not worth noting. The proficiency of the dancing was important, proficiency that could be produced only by those long years at the barre and before the mirror, years that inspired respect for tradition and obedience to its rules. The personality of Legnani seems to have been insignificant, for only her skills are mentioned.

Can we recapture the artworld of the Maryinsky with its elite, conservative audience; its carefully nurtured, somewhat docile dancers; its modular choreography; its reverence for beauty and technical mastery? Some of it we do not even need to recapture, for it is still with us. Though the law of the box office has replaced the rule of the tsar, most ballet tastes remain conservative, and star performers are generally bigger attractions than choreographers. But while the values may have the same names, their meanings differ significantly. The evolution of ballet technique and the accumulated experience of the audience have changed the nature of the feats now acknowledged as brilliant. The body line considered elegant in 1895 appears heavy and insufficiently extended to us now. In addition we place a further demand on the dancers, for—since the advent of Fokine and the modern dance—audiences expect some dramatic expressiveness in performances of narrative works. A "cold" ballerina may be forgiven if her technique is outstanding, but the deficiency is apt to be remarked. Today a star is not only a virtuoso but a personality—a Nureyev, Baryshnikov. While the act of dancing remains central, the nature of what is acclaimed in dancing has greatly changed. To appreciate the "truly authentic" *Swan Lake*—providing, of course, that it could be faithfully revived—we would have to put aside some of our predispositions and assume others. We would have to conceive of dance as the artists and the audience of the Maryinsky conceived it, accepting its conventions and technical standards, preferring airs and graces to actions and passions.

Writing at the end of the eighteenth century, Adam Smith found that the imitative powers of dance were "at least equal, perhaps superior to those of any other art." However, he considered its sphere limited: it was not suitable to the presentation of reasoning or judgment, though it was adept at narrating adventures of love and war or portraying the sentiments, emotions, and passions of the heart. Here, in fact, he found it superior to music, though inferior to poetry. He granted, however, that dance was not necessarily imitative, that it did not have to represent action or character, but that it could still produce "agreeable effects by displaying extraordinary grace and agility." The audience of the Maryinsky, a century later and in another country, seems to have especially approved of Smith's closing thought. And they were not alone, for grace and agility have frequently been cited as characteristic of the best dancing. Could they be the necessary and sufficient causes of dance movement? If not, could they at least suggest the features of a family trait? What about the imitative function that Smith found optional? Can we have a dance that lacks dance movement?

Left: The brilliance of traditional airs and graces is displayed by Suzanne Farrell, shown here with Peter Martins in George Balanchine's *Chaconne. Photo by Martha Swope.*

Above: Untraditional airs and graces are exhibited by the dancers in Merce Cunningham's *Locale*. Left to right: Susan Emery, Rob Remley, Lise Friedman, Alan Good, Catherine Kerr, Joseph Lennon, Ellen Cornfield. *Photo by Nathaniel Tileston.*

Jim May is the embodiment of passion in Anna Sokolow's *Dreams. Photo by Lois Greenfield.*

Dana Reitz rejects both technical and emotional presentation in favor of structural manipulation in *Phrase Collection.* From left: Deborah Gladstein, Jane Comfort, and the choreographer. *Photo by Nathaniel Tileston.*

3. The Girdle of Venus

Sandro Botticelli, "Primavera" (1477–78). Venus and the three graces exhibit the gift of the gods (detail). *Courtesy Editorial Photocolor Archives.*

THE STORY comes from the *Iliad*, but I will use the Roman names, since they are more frequently associated with this particular episode. It begins with the predicament of Juno. She and Jove are having marital problems, but she has a favor to ask of him; the situation, she feels, requires more than tact on her part, and she appeals to Venus for help. Venus, possessor of "all the suavities and charms of love," takes from under her breast a brocaded girdle. "From this come her enchantments: allurement of the eyes, hunger of longing." Wearing the borrowed *kestos* beneath her own bosom, Juno hastens over the mountains, "not touching the ground with her feet," her seduction of Jove assured.

The *kestos* appears again in some versions of the story of the judgment of Paris, when Juno and Minerva demand that Venus remove it because it gives her an unfair advantage in the beauty contest. In the second century A.D., Apuleius described the scene of the goddess's bid: "Venus began placidly to move with hesitating slow step, gently swaying her body, slightly inclining her head, and with delicate gestures responded to the voluptuous sound of the flutes, now with a tender dropping of the eyelids, now with fiery glances." Of course, she won. So motion—especially motion that charms with its ease and fluidity—seems to be intrinsically associated with Venus. When he first beholds her, Aeneas is not certain of her identity, but then she moves "and by her graceful walk a Goddess shows." Grace is found in the moving body.

The graceful Venus has also been described as attended by a trio of graces. To the Greek poet Hesiod in the ninth century B.C., they are dancers of the gods from whom come all graces. The central one is Thalia (verdure), for grace makes the soul bloom. The others are Aglaia (brightness) and Euphrosyne (joy). The fifteenth-century Platonic philosopher Marsilio Ficino identified them with the planets, harmonious companions in "the heavenly dance." He called them Splendour, Youth, and Gladness. Beauty he defined as a grace composed of three graces: Apollo, who attracts the ear with his music; Venus, who attracts the eye with color and shape; Mercury, who attracts the intelligence with the love of divine contemplation. So the graces are identified with the arts and especially with dance, with ordered, beautiful movement.

In Botticelli's "Primavera," the graces are surely dancing. As depicted here, Venus has been variously described as melancholy, laughing, and pregnant, while Ernst Gombrich suggests that she is beating time to the dance of the graces. Venus and two of her attendants (the third has her back to us) wear necklaces that end in pendants; those of the graces lie near the throat, but that of the goddess falls—as the *Iliad* told us it did—just below her breasts.

The placement of the *kestos* is unmistakable in both texts and iconography. The Greeks had good reason to place it there. More than two thousand years later their insight was rediscovered when Isadora Duncan sought "that dance which might be the divine expression of the human spirit through the medium of the body's movement. For hours I would stand quite still, my two hands folded between my breasts, covering the solar plexus. . . . I was seeking, and finally discovered, the central spring of all movement, the crater of motor power, the unity from which all diversions of movements are born . . . the centrifugal force reflecting the spirit's vision."

Though Isadora's religion tended to be of a rather personal nature, her reference to the source of movement as a reflection of spiritual power would have pleased the fourth-century Saint Augustine, who condemned graceful movements that merely pleased the senses but accepted those that pleased the soul, which finds delight by means of the senses. Indeed, Augustine's Christian concept of grace was not entirely alien to the idea embodied in the girdle of Venus, for that too was a gift that transformed the recipient, giving him powers that he could not cultivate by merely human effort. Whether secular or spiritual, grace has been conceived as a treasure offered to the chosen few.

The idea of earthly grace as a mysterious gift did not, however, meet with approval in the early years of the eighteenth, that most rational of centuries. In 1711, the earl of Shaftesbury asserted that some can learn grace from nature while others "as by Reflection, and the assistance of Art, have learnt to form those Motions which on experience are found the easiest and most natural." Perfection of grace he found only in those with a liberal education. As the century wore on, however, thinkers gave less credit to human endeavor as the source of grace and began to revert to the idea of the inscrutable gift. The age of rationalism was drawing to a close.

In Montesquieu's 1757 "Essay on Taste," the girdle of Venus reappeared in a section suggestively titled "Du je ne sais quoi." The *kestos*, contends Montesquieu, has a magical effect; it confers a power to please that seems to come from some invisible source. There is no way for a person to acquire this power, and any conscious effort to simulate it is immediately recognized as affectation. To Montesquieu grace reveals itself as behavior that seems ingenuous and naive; it is free and unconstrained, appearing without obvious cause and therefore characterized in its effect by an element of surprise. This natural charm, this grace, cannot be rationally explained, cannot be properly defined, yet we know what the author means when he calls it the "je ne sais quoi." Two Scottish contemporaries agreed. David Hume described grace as something mysterious and unaccountable. Thomas Reid pronounced it undefinable, though he admitted he knew nothing else that so generally and irresistibly causes love.

Around 1800 Friedrich Schiller set out to probe the secret of the girdle of Venus. Looking at the myth, he concluded that grace is a kind of movable beauty; it is a property that does not belong essentially to its subject but may be produced in it and may disappear from it. The girdle of Venus is the beauty of movement, because movement is the only modification that can affect an object without changing its identity. Schiller also concluded that grace resides only in those voluntary movements that are directed by moral sensibility, since it comes about, not as a result of the practical aim of an action, but from the character of the person who acts. "The subject even ought not to appear to know that it possesses grace. By which we can also see incidentally what we must think of grace, either imitated or learnt (I would willingly call it theatrical grace, or the grace of the dancing master.)"

Also critical of dancers was the nineteenth-century dramatist Heinrich von Kleist, who preferred the movements of animals, because "grace has greater power and brilliance in proportion as the reasoning powers are dimmer and less active." Yet it reappears "when knowledge has . . . passed through infinity." Grace is "at its purest in a body which is entirely devoid of consciousness or which possesses it in an infinite degree; that is, in the marionette or the god."

A gift of Venus, the seductress, or a reflection of virtuous character? Sometimes admired, sometimes condemned; sometimes seen as magical, sometimes subjected to philosophical analysis—grace has fascinated the mind for centuries. And for many of those centuries it has been associated—whether favorably or unfavorably—with the kind of movement referred to as dance. What qualities distinguish movement as graceful? Is graceful movement essential to dance?

Over the years the attribution of some characteristics has been quite consistent, even though, in 1808, Richard Knight claimed that our ideas of grace are "liable to the influence of artificial habits and caprices of fashion." He did, however, admit that one aspect at least is unchanging: grace can exist only in "attitudes and gestures that are naturally appropriate to the constitution of the human body." Reid concurred. After noting that there is no grace without motion, he added that "there can be no grace with impropriety, or that nothing can be graceful that is not adapted to the character and situation of the person."

Grace is also manifested in lightness, and so the heavy body is seldom found to be graceful—though when it is, its grace is especially entrancing because it comes as a surprise. Diderot specified lack of force and delicacy as attributes of grace, expecting that the dancer would also exhibit such contemporary excellences as nobility and precision. The dawn of romantic grace was heralded by Carlo Blasis's call in 1831 for "a sort of abandon," while critics of the following decade compared the lightness of ballerinas to the fluttering of a rose leaf and the flight of a butterfly, as befitted the era of the child of nature. Twentieth-century descriptions have been more analytic than poetic. Raymond Bayer defined reduction of the base of support, as in dancing on pointes, as a source of the impression of lightness. The dancer raises herself until her contact with the floor seems to disappear; grace consists in a prolonged relevé. David Levin in "Balanchine's Formalism" argues that the graceful dancer seems to suspend his earthly self, appears to be weightless, uplifted, released into verticality from his earthbound, horizontal base.

Another persisting attribute is control, a quality easily associated with discipline and consequently—though not necessarily—with virtue. Noting that grace always provokes respect or admiration for the graceful person, Archibald Alison remarked in 1790 that this occurs because grace gives evidence of self-command, the possession of a lofty character governed by high principles that restrain movement. No violent or intemperate gesture can be graceful, and all gestures—regardless of what emotion they express—are graceful if they appear significant of self-command. Grace, indeed, is never evident in movement that lacks composure and temperance, nor in steps that are hurried or disordered as if by anxiety. For Schopenhauer a half century later, grace consists "in every movement being performed and every position assumed, in the easiest and most appropriate and convenient way, and therefore being the pure, adequate expression of its intention, or of the act of will, without any superfluity, which exhibits itself as aimless, meaningless bustle, or as wooden stiffness."

Similarly, Herbert Spencer claimed that grace occurs when a certain action is achieved with the least expenditure of force. The movements of the arms in dancing, he noted, are not simply decorative; on the contrary, they facilitate the general action. Bayer argued that grace involves the suppression of useless, sterile, contagious, involuntary movement; only necessary energy is expended. Nothing moves unless the dancer wants it to move. For Jean-Paul Sartre, grace is the "moving image of necessity and freedom." The hand exists in order to grasp, but it manifests its freedom through the unpredictability of the exact shape of its gesture. Control enables the dancer to quell any unnecessary motion but simultaneously allows a little license in design that does not interfere with the proper rendering of the action. Something more than pure usefulness is involved.

We may well be suspicious, for, despite its efficiency, graceful movement does not look utilitarian. In 1762, Lord Kames attributed grace to motion that is agreeable to the eye apart from any consideration of its appropriateness as a means to an end. A century later, Léon Dumont noted that the Greeks called condiments graces; they were pleasing but unnecessary to nutrition. He admitted that grace can occur in useful movements, however, as long as the manner of accomplishing the task appears to be more important than the result. The notion that grace is generally distinct from practicality has persisted: "Function and grace are combined in this set of four dessert bowls of clear crystal," Bergdorf Goodman's 1979 Christmas catalogue announced triumphantly!

"It may be remark'd," wrote Hogarth in the mid-eighteenth century, "that all useful habitual motions, such as are readiest to serve the necessary purposes of life, are those made up of plain lines . . . graceful movements in serpentine lines are used occasionally, and rather at times of leisure, than constantly applied to every action we make. The whole business of life may be carried on without them, they being properly speaking, only the ornamental part of gesture." Hogarth delighted in the country dance figure known as the hay, its dancers weaving in and out of each other's lines—a most indirect but graceful way to travel in a circle.

Alison agreed. Angular paths, he believed, indicate the presence of an obstruction and so are not pleasing; curved lines, on the contrary, indicate ease, freedom, and playfulness. Most beautiful of all is slow motion in wave like lines—unless the mover is a snake. Spencer suggested that graceful motion is identical with action in curved lines. "Certainly straight or zig-zag movements are excluded from the conception. The sudden stoppages and irregularities which angular movements imply are its antithesis; for a leading element of grace is continuity, flowingness." The cat, noted Ruth St. Denis of nature's most graceful creature, lies down in a series of curves.

Dumont, however, asserted that the shape of the line of movement is not the point, for even the serpentine can become dull. What counts is variety within unity. Without diversity, there is no grace, for the body appears stiff and lifeless, mechanical. To be sure, monotony may have its theatrical uses. Hogarth was pleased by the humor of a new wooden shoe dance: "both the man and the woman often comically fix themselves in uniform positions, and frequently start in equal time, into angular forms." Dumont drew attention to the traditional Pierrot: both arms hanging straight down, all his movements strictly parallel, a most— intentionally—ungraceful character.

Just any mixture of movements, though, will not produce grace. Unity, harmony, and consistency of texture are essential. Such a totality of image was largely underrated by eighteenth-century decorum and Victorian reticence, which allowed the arms and legs a degree of freedom but imprisoned the torso in a tightly protective corset. Knight criticized the prevailing balletic principle that "the body should not feel the movements of the limbs, but remain like an inflexible pillar or barrel." Today, like the romantics, we look for harmony in the figure of the fully vibrant dancer.

Harmony also implies complexity. True, overly complicated movement is difficult to follow and tires the eye, but movement can be so plain that it lacks interest and consequently affords us little pleasure. In 1889 Paul Souriau recommended *"un peu de fantaisie."* Bayer found grace in the dancer's play within a structure, and John Cage elaborated: "Clarity is cold, mathematical, inhuman, but basic and earthy. Grace is warm, incalculable, human, opposed to clarity, and like the air. Grace . . . is used to mean the play with and against clarity of rhythmic structure." In music and dance he found clarity and structure always together, "endlessly and life-givingly, opposed to each other."

Bayer saw the dancer combining steps with such speed and artistry that the eye can not take in all their intricate patterns. Yet the eye is not confused, but rather is fascinated by the intriguing richness of the panorama. Bayer stressed the importance of *broderies*—the petite batterie, the rond de jambe, and especially the fouetté, a true embellishment, with the free leg entwining around the support, like a climbing plant in a serpentine ascent around a still center. He delighted in gratuitous ornamentation, in appoggiaturas. Grace, he declared, is the transfiguration of the mechanics of dance.

Grace delights the viewer, but to varying degrees. A graceful child, skipping along a grassy path, is a pleasure to see; a graceful woman, swaying to music heard in the moonlight, charms the beholder; a graceful dancer, smiling as he manipulates the hazards of a complicated sequence, sets the audience quivering with rapture. Alison remarked that "when we see the dancer move without hurry or disorder; perform all the steps of the dance with ease, accommodate his motions with justice to the measure, and extricate himself from all the apparent intricacies of the figure with order and facility, we feel a very perceptible sentiment of surprise and admiration, and are conscious of the grace of the gestures in which so much skill, and composure, and presence of mind are displayed." Sartre warned that grace ceases when it is successfully thwarted. But the existence of the threat heightens our delight when grace triumphs.

Alison found a higher degree of grace in movements that express serenity and self-possession in cases of danger, but only when "they do not degenerate into tricks of mere agility, or unnatural postures." Dumont, too, warned that the dancer must perform with ease the most perilous jumps, the most astonishing extensions, the most difficult pirouettes, complicated entrechats, extravagant evolutions—and during all this a smile of ease never leaves his lips, for without the appearance of ease he would cease to be graceful, which means he would cease to dance.

Or so they were saying up to the 1930s. After then the notion of grace in dance seems to occur principally in the writings of journalists who can apparently think of nothing more specific to say about last night's ballerina, or in the derogatory remarks of some advocates of contemporary experimental dance who find grace anachronistic. What happened? Is grace no longer necessary?

What happened by the thirties was, of course, the dramatic modern dance. The new choreographers had read Freud and Frazer and had sought the psychic truths behind the ancient myths. With expression of inner feeling as their primary goal and with small concern for Fokine's concept of idealization, they cared little for grace of movement as a quality to compel attention. They eschewed such epithets as "dainty," "delicate," and especially "ethereal," because their point was—in Martha Graham's apt phrase— to exhibit "the miracle that is a human being." Down with fairies. The perfect achievement of flight was not possible to the human being, though he could aspire to it, albeit without hope of getting very far. More appropriate were qualities of tension, of struggle, of limited accomplishment. But the victory appeared the more monumental because it was achieved in spite of visible obstacles. The conventional ballet dancer of that period was supposed to move as if the most basic mortal barriers did not exist for him. The concept involved an oversimplification of the classical balletic style, but it accounted for some aspects of the revolt of the moderns. Was grace, then, completely out?

Even in the modern dance some of it remained. To express emotion, to call attention to the feeling of the character portrayed, still demanded the control associated with grace. To be dramatically compelling on stage, the dancer cannot allow involuntary movement to distract the viewer. The obstacles revealed must be only those that the choreographer wants to be seen. What degree of effort should be visible to convince the audience of the performer's humanity is also limited and subject to control. The law of economy continued to operate, though sylphlike lightness was no longer desirable. Elegance and ornamentation had to go at this time, also, but the performer had to possess skill, and in some ways that skill was even more demanding, for in the days of the early modern dance a display of technical expertise would have been considered decadent; the deftness had to be there but it had to be hidden. The freedom that comes from mastery had to be there too, though not to allow for decorative flourishes. Rather, freedom from physical concerns was needed so that the dancer could concentrate on dramatic interpretation. The idea was to show fear of the jealous lover or of fate, but not fear of losing the balance on an arabesque.

Then at midcentury Merce Cunningham turned away from drama to work with manipulations of movement for its own sake. If the actions of the dancer did not have to be expressive, a wide range of possibilities became available. As far as appearance was concerned, grace in its various traditional senses was neither demanded nor prohibited; it could be appropriate to some ways of exploring movement and not to others. Of course some of the invisible qualities of grace were needed; control was essential if the dancer was not to distort the movement qualities that were the essence of what Cunningham wanted to display. But the choreographer had only occasional use for lightness, made considerable use of straight lines, and—because he favored chance over emotional continuity—frequently presented movement that was fragmented rather than flowing. Nor was Cunningham interested in broderies; he was more concerned with uncluttered, subtle variations and juxtapositions of lines and textures that could be distinctly perceived. "Grace," he once said, "comes when the energy for the given situation is full and there is no excess." To illustrate, he cited Julia Child in the kitchen.

The events of the 1960s presented another kind of blow to conventional grace, for then the idea was to utilize ordinary movement, even to utilize nondancers. Costuming emphasized the everyday, anti-illusionistic concept: women wore no makeup; both sexes dressed in slacks and sneakers; occasionally the choreographer voiced instructions to the performers as if to assure the audience that preparations had been perfunctory. Of course, some control was exerted, but it was largely concealed. Alison would have found it dull, for there was no display to trigger admiration or surprise, but the point was to minimize the elitist distinction between performer and audience. Instead of feeling wonder at the skills of creatures unlike themselves, the observers were to feel that the performers were really only people like themselves. The dance was an occasion for the mutual celebration of ordinary movement. The ideas were consistent with the lifestyle of the hippie generation.

The next decade brought other changes as the "modern" dancers began to frequent ballet classes, apparently eager for the most rigorous technical training they could find. As a result, they were not likely to continue to settle for performing in works that asked nothing of their skills, even if they did not think of them as consequences of the freedom bestowed by grace. Nor were choreographers likely to let such skills lie unused. Still, for some, there was no desire to return to nineteenth-century bravura; other guidelines were found, one of them the modernity of a look that was casual and spontaneous. Twyla Tharp sauntered onto the stage, body slouched, arms hanging loosely, as if she were heading for the local bistro after a hard day's work. But the feet and legs were engaged in the most complex maneuvers—incredibly swift changes of weight and direction, sudden shifts in dynamics and rhythmic patterns. These required control. The body moved with fluidity and it looked free, artless, though not particularly elegant, dignified, or light. It was not called graceful because by now the term had taken on connotations that never belonged to it before: simpering, affected, fussy. The word had become, and remains, somewhat suspect.

Yet we continue to admire those aspects of the real grace that pertain even to contemporary dance: control, precision, freedom, the appearance of spontaneity, flow. And we continue to admire the balletic skill that enables the dancer to exhibit these qualities in the face of mounting choreographic demands. Graceful is almost inadequate to describe the fleet passage of the Balanchine dancer through a series of intricate broderies or in the suave conquest of a long and ornate configuration of traveling steps. The mastery goes by practically unnoticed because other considerations have taken precedence—elegance of line, subtlety of phrasing, musicality. The concept keeps changing.

What was the state of grace in 1895 St. Petersburg? The reviewers of *Swan Lake*, as we have seen, praised Legnani for hers, noting the confidence and ease of her performance. Of the other qualities previously attributed to grace, natural charm had apparently lost its appeal; the critics of the romantic ballet had delighted in the illusion of artlessness and spontaneity displayed by their sylphs, but a half century later it was brilliance and precision—no matter how calculated—that seemed more important. We may recall the association of grace with self-command achieved through discipline, and this was much valued by the Maryinsky. The eighteenth-century concept of grace is also reflected in a contemporary homage to Ivanov for his dances that exhibited "the noble imprint of a dignified style." Still, the well-rounded figures and obviously muscular legs of many of the ballerinas hardly suggested the traditional delicacy of grace.

More and more often in this period the praises are bestowed on the grace that masters technical challenge. Legnani may have acted as if no difficulty existed for her, but the audience—many of them knowledgeable in the ways of the ballet classroom—recognized the threat and knew where to applaud the victory. Karsavina, admitting that Legnani's fouettés were "not unlike an acrobatic exercise," nevertheless conceded that "the feat as she performed it, had something elemental and heroic in its breathless daring." Here we have met the counterpart of grace: virtuosity.

Top left: Traditional grace—curves, lightness, elegance. Merrill Ashley in George Balanchine's *Ballo dalla Regina*. *Photo by Martha Swope.*

Left: A contemporary alternative—angles and earthy energy. Ze'eva Cohen in Frances Alenikoff's "The One of No Way." *Photo by Jack Mitchell.*

Above: Also contemporary—weighted nonchalance. From left: Sara Rudner, Rose Marie Wright, and Twyla Tharp in Tharp's "Eight Jelly Rolls." *Photo by Tony Russell, London Weekend Television, Ltd.*

The body that lacks harmony lacks grace. Larry Grenier as
the transformed Bottom in the Joffrey Ballet production of
Frederick Ashton's *The Dream. Photo by Herbert Migdoll.*

4. The Achieve of, the Mastery of the Thing!

Drawing by B. Petty; © *1965*
The New Yorker Magazine, Inc.

VIRTUOSITY, epitomizing the dancer's mastery of the ordinary impediments to human movement, is a palpitation of the heart for the fan and a pain in the neck for the theorist. "Wow!" screams the aficionado as the dancer leaps (after performing a far more difficult feat of balance quite unnoticed by the audience). "But my dear," intones the purist, "there was no dramatic motivation for that display. Simply playing to the gallery."

"Brava!" shrieks the watcher of the thirty-two fouettés, which Fokine termed "the most hateful invention of the ballet." He wrote those words in 1916; in 1942 he choreographed *Bluebeard*—which included a passage of thirty-two fouettés.

Does virtuosity lie in the actual skill demanded by the movement or in the appearance of skill? Can virtuosity serve drama or will it necessarily distract the viewer from more "serious" concerns? Is virtuosity today still virtuosity tomorrow? Is virtuosity necessary? Is virtuosity even—good?

Despite its persisting popularity, balletic virtuosity has had a goodly share of detractors. In the sixteenth century when ballet began, the problem was basically quiescent, since the weight of the dancers' costumes, along with their comparatively meagre skills and the prevailing mores, constrained them from the performance of pyrotechnics. But in the eighteenth century, when the ballet was taken over by professionals, proficiency increased, the public discovered the delights of virtuosity, and dancers discovered the pleasures of applause. As early as 1712, however, complaints were heard in London. John Weaver objected in both writing and choreography, but the opinions of Sir Richard Steele reached a wider audience. Urging that dance was not really a trivial art, Steele begged his readers to disdain "such impertinents as fly, hop, caper, tumble, twirl, turn round, and jump over their Heads, and, in a word, play a thousand Pranks which many Animals can do better than a Man."

Nevertheless, it was not long before dancers learned to accomplish such complicated maneuvers as only human ingenuity could contrive. Before 1800 Marie Camargo had done her entrechat quatre and Anna Heinel her double pirouette. Yet neither would attract much attention today, for part of the appeal of virtuosity lies in its novelty. As familiarity lessens the delight, feats of virtuosity quickly become dated. (This can happen in the course of a single evening, as I noticed at a performance that produced thirty-two fouettés on three successive occasions—the last an utter bore.) Fortunately, however, virtuosity long forgotten can sometimes be rediscovered and made to evoke its magic afresh, as happened in the 1950s when the world outside Denmark caught its first glimpse of the Royal Danish Ballet and was newly enchanted by its ballon and delicate batterie.

Detractors claim that virtuosity has a transient effect and that bravura is not worthy of a great art, which should rely on qualities that provide more lasting pleasures. Yet many spectators remember the thrills of a spectacle of virtuosity long after the details of a dramatic performance have faded from memory. What precisely has made them remember? Is it the same ingredient that makes the sports fan recall that beautiful swan dive? Or that great home run? Or have we encountered some differences in species of stellar excitement?

The virtuoso dancer is often accused of usurping the territory of the athlete, stressing quantity instead of quality, for aiming to set a numerical record rather than presenting a persona to charm the audience with its beauty or move it with an emotional portrayal. The distinction was drawn by T. S. Eliot: "The acrobat, however bad or good, appeals to the mind rather than to the senses. We admire his *skill*, we say, that is difficult; and we could not do it—or we are pleased by *mere* surprise or novelty. . . . There are acrobats, such as Rastelli, whose juggling appeals to our sense of beauty of form; but his is an added gift. The primary appeal of acrobatics is to the mind. You must have the skill or you cannot produce this effect; but the appreciation of skill is for the trained critic alone, not for the general audience." Eliot would say, then, that the quantitative aspect of virtuosity (the balleto-manes at the Maryinsky counting up to thirty-two to be sure that Legnani had made it) should be subordinated to the attraction of its form.

Today's writers on the aesthetics of sport usually agree with Eliot that beauty in athletics is a by-product, not essential to the successful accomplishment of the designated act. However, some of them (such as David Best) distinguish between purposive and aesthetic sports. The former, like baseball, are rule-dominated and goal-directed; the purposive athlete is concerned with effi-ciency and results, his achievements are objectively measurable. But some sports are more concerned with manner than with end result; their emphasis on appearance, form, and style brings such sports as gymnastics and ice skating close to the realm of dance. The problem has been complicated, however, since the institution of ballet competitions in Varna in 1964, though here—unlike the Olympics—each judge is allowed to set his own criteria and to award points in terms of his individual standards.

Benjamin Lowe has cited several principles that should guide the athlete: he must be governed by real properties of space, time, and mass; his use of these elements must be efficient and within the rules of the game. The gymnast can be somewhat creative in his phrasing, but his movements are set. The dancer, however, "expands on time and space, limited only by a personal limitation of body mass, and uses energy extravagantly to maximize emo-tional involvement." (Apparently, Lowe did not consider the danc-er "limited" by the choreography.) "We do not dance," noted Straus, "to get from one point to another in space . . . the dance is not goal directed . . . we move *through* space from one point to another; dancing, we move *within* space." Curious about the possibility of combining the efficiency of athletic movement with the rhythm and design of dance, Charles Moulton has created a series of "precision ball passing" dances that serve the demands of both the sport and the art.

Referring to the theatrical shift of temporality, Denby has contrasted dance-time and "everyday time," while Rudolf Arnheim asked about the dancer's leap: "Is it an aspect of our experience, let alone the most significant aspect, that time passes during the leap? Does she arrive out of the future and jump through the present into the past? Obviously not. . . . We simply witness an event unrolling, unfolding in a sensible order." For dance, both performer and audience shift into a special time-space dimension. This is not the case with sport.

In sport, said Lowe, the expressive function is subordinate. He proceeded to list the primary qualities by which athletic movement can be judged: they are grace, rhythm, control, lightness, speed, risk, precision, power, "joy of effort," and strategy. These apply to technical performance, but Lowe recognized also a symbolic level of performance, one that is resonant of ethical values and social behavior. For him, sport achieves its greatest triumphs when emotional content is more striking to the observer than purely technical action.

Not all writers accept such a symbolic level; many are willing to settle for a version closer to Danto's theory that in the case of artworks "it makes sense, as it does not with mere real objects, to ask what they are *of* or are *about*." Best argued that a proper art form "must at least allow for the possibility of the artist's comment, through his art, on life situations and this is not possible in diving, skating, trampolining and gymnastics." While Best was willing to grant aesthetic values to sports, he was not willing to accept them as art forms. He admitted that current trends in abstract painting and dance present "difficult cases," but he did not grapple with some of the basic problems this raised. If a choreographer renounces his opportunity to comment, does he thereby renounce his function as an artist? How does the diver make that suspension in the air so thrilling? Only because he has mastered a skill? Or perhaps because, like the dancer, he has shown that a mere human can challenge and conquer—at least to a remarkable degree—some of the normally constraining forces of nature?

Louis Arnaud Reid noted that games may "express" such feelings as relieved tension and aggression, "but they do not, as art does, present or represent these transformed in embodied form for contemplation." In saying this, however, he referred to a restricted area of sports. When he got to gymnastics, Reid softened the distinction, suggesting that, once mastery had been attained, the gymnast can will to be something of an artist; even within the rules "he is freed to give the movement expressive form, which is his own creation, and which is meaning-embodied." Still Reid did not call gymnastics an art; it has artistic elements, but this is not its dominating purpose; therefore it is not art. Would a change in purpose that is unknown to the audience make the difference between nonart and art? If I turn on the television set in the middle of a program and if the bottom of the picture is cut off and I don't see the skates, if I just see people moving beautifully in time and space—what would lead me to conclude that this is not art?

Thus, many of the qualities admired in both athletics and dance sound familiar from the preceding chapter; the acrobat has, in fact, been defined as one who joins grace to strength of muscles. Generally, though, strength is not associated with grace; on the contrary, the graceful action is thought of as soft, gentle, delicate. Can strength and grace coexist? While the athlete may want to conceal his true anxiety under a surface of composure, of assured self-control, he is under less compulsion to hide his effort; unlike the dancer, he seldom finds cause to smile in the course of his work. In most sports the athlete displays his strength, his weight; forcefulness, not softness, is a desirable quality. No football player wants to look like a pussycat; he would prefer to resemble a tiger, as would the male dancer, and here the dividing line becomes narrow indeed. But we may look further.

We applaud the grace of the dancer who overcomes a technical difficulty, but not if he stresses the difficulty to the point of our being aware of the presence of fear. With the athlete we want to be especially alert to the danger, to applaud his courage sometimes even more than his skill. A certain visible tension in the performance can heighten this—as can the absence of a net below the circus trapeze. Lowe suggested that the aesthetic experience is intensified in proportion to the greatness of the handicap, and we remarked that the effect of grace was enhanced when it was threatened. But there may be a limit. Sometimes the acrobatic feat looks so dangerous, so lethally menacing, that we can hardly bear to watch it. This would defeat the point of dance virtuosity, which should rivet our attention, not with fear, but with delight. Deborah Jowitt has noted the difference between the dancer as stuntman and the dancer as celestial acrobat—an important distinction.

How does the audience know what is difficult if the performer does not give the clue with a frown or a heave of the chest? In his discussion of musical virtuosity Thomas Mark has warned that the display of skill in an artwork is not obvious to untutored contemplation: "being a product of skill is not a directly perceivable property of the artworks that have it. This means that appreciation of works of virtuosity, in which display of skill is central, presupposes some knowledge."

In discussing these skills Mark draws most of his examples from music, which leads him to some conclusions that he might have qualified if he had looked at dance. For anyone who has never attempted to play the piano, a virtuoso passage may well go unnoticed. With the dancer, however, our contact is of a different kind; most often we need no program notes to tell us that a body like our own has vanquished gravity or vertigo. A primal human instinct is at work here; the desire to defy gravity, to fly through the air, to spin in space without succumbing to dizziness, to maintain the equilibrium while barely touching the earth. Our reactions to comparable feats executed by other bodies are not the same.

We gaze in wonder at the graceful cabriole of the Lippizaner horse, at the dolphin's majestic leap from the depths of the sea to high in the air. We applaud, we sense a measure of affinity with these marvelous creatures, but kinesthetically we do not leap with them. Gerard Manley Hopkins was stirred by the ecstatic flight of a bird: "the achieve of, the mastery of the thing!" But he watched it from afar, with his heart "in hiding," a mere human in awe of this feathered conqueror. While we share some physical features with dolphins and birds, we cannot experience with them the same degree of sympathetic consciousness that we can experience with our own kind. With the dancer our response is intuitive, and the heart—not hiding but identifying—soars with the performer.

The kinesthetic response is not, however, infallible. Frequently instances of intricate coordination pass unnoticed, while extended adagio sequences—often requiring extraordinary control—tend to be viewed as lyrical rather than brilliant by all but the connoisseur. They do, indeed, presuppose some knowledge on the part of the observer. This also holds true for historical works that display feats of virtuosity that no longer impress us because they have become commonplace. The dancer impersonating the early eighteenth-century Marie Camargo approaches center stage, smiles at her late twentieth-century audience, flicks her wrists expectantly, bends her knees a little, and executes—a single entrechat quatre. Will anyone applaud? Nowadays audiences seldom get excited about sixteen entrechats six. Program notes would help, but there is no guarantee that everyone would read them. Sometimes the creation of the proper technical context can accustom the unknowing eye to the restrained smallness and evenness of the period style so that, by contrast, the entrechat quatre will appear at least ingenious if not actually brilliant. As fouettés become increasingly common, the problem of the lessening glitter of Odile's tour de force will demand further consideration.

Mark defines works of virtuosity: they require skills, they are about the skills that they require, and they display the skills they are about. Here the skills referred to are those of composition, and the only dance instance that comes clearly to my mind is Frederick Ashton's *Scènes de Ballet*, a positively virtuosic application of the figures of Euclidean geometry to the art of choreography. Mark distinguishes these works from those that have the virtuosity of performance as their subject matter and are so constructed that a proper performance of them must necessarily be itself a work of virtuosity. He cites the Chopin études, and for dance any number of bravura pas de deux might be placed in this category, though I know of only one complete ballet, Harald Lander's—not incidentally titled *Etudes*—that seems comparable.

As I write this, though, the word going around town is that Paul Taylor's new *Arden Court* has performance virtuosity as its subject. Undoubtedly, it requires skills and it displays those skills, but at the same time aspects of the choreography suggest that it might be about something else. Taylor admitted that the duets "are based on quasi-emotional situations. . . . There is fast circling of a slow mover, with the implications of lover and beloved." His dancer Carolyn Adams felt a less precise significance in the dichotomy, "a difference in *states*," while my own impression tended toward a still center and a turning world. *Arden Court* requires virtuosity for its performance, but it is not about virtuosity; to claim that is to miss a part of its message.

Feats of virtuosity may, in fact, occur in works that are about something else entirely, that make no attempt to exhibit skills for their own sake. The expressive modern dancers of the 1930s and 1940s performed in works that were full of intrinsic difficulties, but they were not seen in works of virtuosity. The skills were there, but not as the subject of the works; they were the means to dramatic statements. Graham's back fall was a miraculous product of strength and control: the body—impelled by grief—noiselessly dropped to the ground, filling the observer not with admiration for the dancer but with pity for the character. With José

Limón a leap was no statement of personal power; it was a noble act of will: a creature of the earth, knowing that aspiration was ultimately futile, nevertheless endeavored to reach for glory. With visible effort he raised himself into the air. There was no applause, nor should there have been.

Today the image for some choreographers is deliberately pedestrian. The key is antivirtuosity. The appeal is to the kind of person who does not desire to soar above the crowd but to be one of it. Sally Banes notes that, beginning in the 1960s, "there was freedom to express all the faux pas dancers must repress and mask in 'normal' performance—such as stumbling or forgetting . . . they ate, hummed, walked away from a group activity, explained to the audience what was going on." There was freedom to stumble, but there was no freedom to shine in a bravura feat. Marcia Siegel has suggested that such dancers appeared as people "like us almost." But this was not the exclusive image of the time. Arlene Croce, reviewing Balanchine's dancers of that decade, remarked that they "have no age—they're divine."

According to the standards of Edward Bullough the choreographers of the postmodern dance err by erasing the aesthetic distance between the audience and themselves, while Balanchine rightly maintains it. Bullough believed that awareness of distance was necessary to aesthetic appreciation. The theatre generally is vulnerable in this respect, because the very physical presence of the performers tends to narrow the gap; they seem too much "like us almost." In what he called the "higher forms of dancing," Bullough found that "technical execution of the most wearing kind makes up a great deal for its intrinsic tendency toward a loss of Distance." Paul Bouissac has analyzed the solution to the problem as proposed by the circus acrobat who accentuates his difference from the audience with a costume that erases the outlines of his muscles, and with his smile, his courtly mode of social behavior. Most important, of course, is his display of technical accomplishment which, with its expertly hidden mechanics, demonstrates his biological superiority to the mere mortals who observe him. Display of virtuosity would seem to achieve the same kind of goal for dance. But Balanchine's ballets generally do not display virtuosity.

Most of the works of Balanchine do not exhibit the skills of his dancers, do not frame the feats of technical prowess for the audience to admire, but rather absorb them in what Denby called a "continuity of impetus." The ongoing momentum, the steady flow of phrasing, envelop the potentially bravura passages so that they are not isolated for exhibition (barring a deliberate touch of vulgarity as in *Stars and Stripes*). The dancers remain distinct from the audience because their movements seem determined only by the choreographic form, untouched by the exigencies of the real world. Balanchine's ballets use skill but they are not about skill; they are about Valéry's "most subtle essence of music and movement"; they are about the "state of dancing."

At the opposite end of the scale, what about dancing that appears virtuosic but is not intrinsically difficult because it is produced by hidden means—by subterfuge, you might say. Is it fair? Is it still art? When Marie Taglioni first danced *La Sylphide* in 1832, her choreographer father wanted her to fly, so he resorted to the use of wires. Charles-Louis Didelot had already done it in *Flore et Zéphire* in 1796, and as it would serve Filippo Taglioni's purpose without unduly taxing his daughter, why not? The audience knew that the wires were being used; they might even have tried to see them through the dim lighting of the scene; on the other hand, they might have been so carried away by the tragic fate of the sylphide that they did not even think to try to discern the wires.

Another case: Gloria Gilbert, billed as the Human Top, astonished audiences some years ago by spinning twenty or so pirouettes on pointe from a single preparation. Did she? Yes, she did have ball bearings in the tips of her toe shoes. She also had very good balance or she could never have carried it off. But that's all she had and that's all she did—she turned. I saw her in a

Chicago Theatre stage show and I seem to remember everything I saw as a teenager, but I have never met anyone else who remembered Gloria Gilbert. Everyone who saw her remembered Taglioni.

By now the status of the toe shoe is fairly well known: several layers of stiffening fill in the tip of the dainty pink satin slipper, enabling the dancer to accomplish feats of balance impossible—well, practically impossible—to her romantic forebears, who settled for a bit of darning for reinforcement. Is this modern, artificial box fair? Is it important that the audience know about this material aid? Why should the toe shoe be considered any more legitimate than ball bearings?

The usefulness of ball bearings is limited: they permit the execution of multiple turns and that's it. But the uses of toe shoes are myriad: they facilitate the performance of a number of steps, because the reduction of surface contact with the floor enables the dancer to move more smoothly and faster; they also provide her with a wide range of movement qualities, from delicate skimming over the stage to sharp taqueté attack. The use of pointes extends the line of the dancer so that she may be seen in an unbroken vertical configuration from head to toe. The use of pointes can distinguish feminine from masculine, aerial from earthly creatures. Pointe shoes extend the scope of the dancer's skills. They aid virtuosity but they do not create it. When they are properly used, the audience admires the artistry of the performer, not the craftsmanship of Capezio.

More important than the means are the functions of virtuosity. Take those fouettés, for example. In David Lichine's *Graduation Ball* they form part of a competition; as audience we commit no artistic crime if we count them or gasp at some unusual spectacular variation. That is exactly what they are about. But the statistical approach to the fouettés in *Swan Lake* is another matter. Shouldn't they make a dramatic contribution to the proceedings? Some say that Odile uses them to dazzle the prince (though he is usually offstage—probably preparing for his own grand jetés—when she performs them). Natalia Makarova believes they signify Odile's already accomplished triumph. Whichever the interpretation, they had better be brilliant. If the ballerina falters or looks frightened, she destroys the characterization and the dramatic point. But if she does something so technically astonishing that the audience starts to wonder, "How did she do that?" then she has again destroyed the effect. In either case, we are brought sharply back to reality; removed from the threatening evil that Odile represents, we find ourselves observing—a dancer with a trick or two up her tutu.

Fokine hated the fouetté of his day because, since it was such a novelty, it was bound to distract the audience from any thoughts of drama. He objected to it also because it was so difficult that the dancer had to step out of character to set all her attention on the accomplishment of the physical task. But in 1942 when Fokine choreographed *Bluebeard*, the thirty-two fouettés were no longer a novelty to the audience and they held no terrors for Irina Baronova. As Bluebeard's sixth wife—and, she hoped, his last—Baronova cornered Alicia Markova, who seemed headed for the status of number seven, whipping her across the stage in a series of thirty-two furious fouettés. These were not about skill; they were about jealousy.

According to Nicolas Giuduci, Vladimir Jankélévitch claims that musical virtuosity is self-inflating—faster, still faster, infinitely faster. Historically each achievement extends the point at which the feat can thrill. As the artist adds more onto more, he tries to give his act cosmic dimension, but actually this attempt is futile, for sheer multiplicity leads only to homogenization. The limit becomes the norm, quality is submerged in quantity, and the result is decadence.

What can determine the boundary? We may thrill to thirty-two fouettés, but as they approach sixty-four they begin to bore us. Wisely, dancers have chosen not to increase the number; the music may have determined this choice, of course, but a sympathetic conductor might have been persuaded to comply. The dancers knew better. Instead of quantity, they added ornamentation. So we have had such variations as single, single, triple; or fouetté, pirouette à la seconde, pirouette en attitude, fouetté; or gradual acceleration (Lupe Serrano's fantastic progression went from seeming slow motion to breakneck speed); or changing spot (two facing front, two facing right, and so on). Lastly—so far in my experience—is Yoko Ichino's innovation: four fouettés, then a swoop into a low arabesque penchée and two slow revolutions holding that pose. Brilliant for the contest in *Graduation Ball*, but too distractingly startling for Odile in *Swan Lake*.

Sheer multiplication, however, will not do anywhere. As early as 1825 August Baron was complaining: a corps of thirty dancers do six pirouettes each, six times—they give us one thousand and eighty pirouettes—a sight to exhaust the best of eyes! I must, nevertheless, make something of an exception for Harald Lander's *Etudes*—a work of virtuosity if ever there was one. Here the number of fouettés is held to sixteen, but five dancers perform them. The demand for synchronization, added to the already considerable demands of the pirouettes, adds a special dimension to the sequence, beyond the matter of quantity. The problem with mere quantity? The action comes to appear mechanical; the sense of personal mastery is lost and with it the observer's delight in the perception of human conquest.

The fouettés occur within a context, whether that context is a story, a mood, or a stylistic statement. This means that a sense of proportion must prevail, the event must take place within a form. Yet virtuosity tends to be personal and frequently exuberant as well—qualities that rebel against the restrictions of form. Part of the excitement of virtuosity stems from this tension. Confidence, ambition, and euphoria strain against the limits imposed by the choreography. There are just so many counts of music; the phrase ends and that beautifully poised balance had better end with it. Or the problem may be characterization, the performer tempted to intrude on the role. Do we applaud Odile or Miss Z portraying Odile?

Jankélévitch noted a point at which virtuosity can achieve the status of a symbol of the eternal struggle of man against the threats of time, space, and chance. Because the spectator longs to conquer these too, and has imagined doing so, the effect is magical, the vociferous reaction spontaneous. The pianist's skill is focused on speed, but the modes of dance virtuosity are more numerous. The dancer conquers time, not only with swift batterie, but with prolonged balances; he triumphs over space in the broad jetés with which he covers the stage, but he vanquishes gravity in the height of his cabrioles.

My favorite defender of dance virtuosity as symbol is Akim Volynsky, though I must take exception to his making the highest form of it the province of the man. Volynsky sees the epitome of virtuosity in elevation where spiritual aspiration shines through the merely animal desire to attain a practical goal. The dancer seems to reach for a utopian realm; his flight courts catastrophe; he is awe-struck by his vision, but bold and daring. Heroically obsessed, he appears transfigured. Transfiguration, adds Volynsky, always requires height (and he seems to mean this both literally and figuratively). No transfigurations occur over a cup of tea, though they may take place with a glass of wine, which can make the spirits soar. The dancer who is not transfigured in flight, who does not exult in high places, lacks artistic fire. The true classic dance is exultation. This desire to soar upward (again both literally and figuratively) is natural to the human being, which accounts for our understanding and feeling of soaring along with the dancer.

Volynsky adds a further point: without this aspiration, without what he calls the "willed awareness of the mountain peak," the leap had better be performed in the circus, jumping over chairs or over people's heads, because it only astonishes by its skill and cannot affect the heart. That we will never actually attain that mountain peak is of no consequence; the dream is within us and it accounts for our response to true virtuosity. Valéry remarked that "the Fates have decreed that among the things indispensable to the race of men, there must figure some insensate desires."

Leaping dolphins. *Photo by Nicki Clancey, Sea Life Park, Makapuu Oceanic Center, Waimanalo, Hawaii.*

Leaping pirate. Mikhail Baryshnikov interprets the old classic *Le Corsair*. *Photo by Martha Swope.*

Charles Moulton's *Three Person Precision Ball Passing.*
Left to right: Gabrielle Lansner, Janna Jensen, and the
choreographer. *Photo by Patti Perret.*

5. *What does the "Dance of the Sugar Plum Fairy" Mean?*

A phrase from the dance in Labanotation. © *1957 Dance Notation Bureau, Inc.*

Alicia Markova is a classically elegant sugar plum fairy. Photo by Maurice Seymour. *Courtesy Dance Collection, The New York Public Library.*

THIS WAS THE question I once asked in the course of an article, and a learned gentleman wrote to tell me that indeed he thought it did mean something, so I wrote back to ask him what did he think it meant. That was several years ago, and I'm still waiting for his answer.

Of course, the dancer in Ivanov's *The Nutcracker* "represents" a sugar plum fairy; we know this because that is what she is called in the program. Would we know it otherwise? How does the dancer resemble such a creature? Visually she is not like a real sugar plum. She is not round, and furthermore she moves, which candy does not. Does she portray, embody, certain qualities associated with sugar plums? Gooey? No. Sweet? Perhaps, but not in quite the same way. Is she just a vision of "everything nice"? If so, her qualities are vaguely similar to those of just about all other "nice" fairies. What is distinctive about a sugar plum fairy? Would we know one if we saw her in the street?

Perhaps we had better try another kind of approach. What clues does the story provide for us? Asleep under the Christmas tree, little Clara dreams that she and her Nutcracker Prince are guests of honor at a party in the Kingdom of Sweets, the domain of the Sugar Plum Fairy. This charming hostess provides an entertainment for her guests: dances by Chocolate, Tea, Coffee, and Marzipan are climaxed by the "Waltz of the Flowers." The hostess now does her solo variation and then, with a cavalier who has conveniently appeared, she does a lovely pas de deux. Finally a sleigh arrives to carry Clara back to the real world.

Does this help? Not much. The qualities of character needed by the plot are minimal; as long as the fairy is generally amiable in her manner she would fit the requirements. Can we discern any more from the choreography?

To the bell-like sounds of the celesta, the dancer starts to cross the stage on a diagonal path, taking gently accented steps on her toes as her free leg softly bends and straightens. She then does a little run on her toes, beats one foot lightly and quickly several times against the other, and does a quarter of a turn, ending with one leg extended to the back. This is repeated to the other side (in fact, most of her phrases are done first to the right and then to the left, creating a neatly symmetrical pattern). Other movements include small jumps, never covering very much space, and steps that take her into a variety of poses on the toes of one foot, all closely marking the staccato accents and phrases of the music. Though requiring considerable strength and control, these movements look soft but their yielding quality is balanced by a sharp clarity of focus; the dancer seems always aiming at a particular position in space, which, once attained, is held just long enough for the viewer to take it in and admire it. She does not force her way to the position; her movements are unhurried. She seems poised and confident, yet gracious.

But surely these qualities could be depicted in a briefer dance. There seems to be no need for all the repeated phrases, for all the measures of steps that appear to say no more than the ones already performed. Why so much movement to say so little? We are reminded of Beardsley's "overflow of expressiveness"; there is simply more action than can be logically justified as necessary to portray the very elementary situation. Furthermore, almost any generally gracious dance would seem to serve the plot and the character of the hostess as well. Is the title purely arbitrary? Does the dance really represent a specific kind of creature? Does a dance have to represent anything?

True, Aristotle noted that the dancer "imitates men's characters as well as what they do and suffer." But since his time other possibilities have been proposed. The most prominent suggestion has come from Susanne Langer. For her the art of dance is "a free symbolic form, which may be used to convey *ideas* of emotion, of awareness and premonition." Her extended argument, intended to disprove the idea that such gestures are actually self-expressive, need not detain us here, for the dancer who portrays the Sugar Plum Fairy (like most theatrical dancers) is simply executing the steps she was given; these are what she must perform regardless of the nature of her personal feelings at the moment. But what, in fact, are the ideas of emotion that she conveys? In this case it seems difficult to pinpoint an exact feeling, though we might specify a disposition of pleasantly warm friendliness. Langer, however, specifies *ideas* of emotion, of human feeling, "the rhythms and connections, crises and breaks, the complexity and richness of what is sometimes called man's 'inner life'." Rhythms and connections are certainly present in the Ivanov variation, though we may look in vain for crises and complexity. The dance is smooth and flowing, the genial disposition portrayed barely fluctuates beyond the ebb and flow of the even musical phrasing. Langer asserts that the "feeling of the whole work is the 'meaning' of the symbol, the reality which the artist has found in the world and of which he wants to give his fellow men a clear conception." But isn't this claiming rather much for a dance of a simply friendly sugar plum fairy?

To be sure, there are dance works that present us with profound ideas (the futility of war in Kurt Jooss's *The Green Table*, the struggle for self-understanding in Graham's *Clytemnestra*, though in Langer's terms only the latter would qualify as concerning the "inner life"). There seem also to be a number of works that have stood the test of time though they offer us little in the way of ideas or go to apparently excessive lengths to say very little (three acts of *Sleeping Beauty* to claim that good will triumph and evil will be banished, which we have heard before). Perhaps the definition of subject matter and theme does not tell the whole story.

Can't a dance just *be*? Simply exist to be enjoyed for the pleasure of our remarking the relationships of movement to music, of the constantly changing yet somehow consistent patterns traced in space, for the delight of seeing the leg slowly unfolding in a développé and then—sharply—both feet closing crisply on pointe, staccato and legato complementing one another? Isn't this "meaning" enough—the cadence, the control, the sense of achieved design?

Perhaps our feeling of disappointment with a dance that seems to lack such formal harmony and structure comes from our suspicion that it also lacks meaning. If the tone is unclear, if the movements look either muddled or monotonous, if the sequence seems arbitrary, we tend to think that the choreographer had nothing to say. Today we do not necessarily ask him to tell us a story, nor do we always seek a momentous message in his work, but we do expect him, in a way, to "speak" to us. If we can discern no reason for his putting together these particular steps in this particular way, we are apt to be disturbed by the absence of personal comment. If, on the contrary, we perceive an individual point of view that tinges all the movements and orders their arrangement, then we may feel that a statement has been made. Some societies, however, would not accept this idea of meaning.

R. G. Collingwood asserted that "dance is the mother of all languages . . . a language in which every movement and every stationary poise of every part of the body had the same kind of significance which movements of the vocal organs possess in a spoken language." How much of prehistoric dance was really so specifically meaningful we will never know, for no society exists that has remained completely unchanged. What we do know is that many tribal societies use dance to convey messages of significance—whether to the gods, asking for rain, or to a neighboring group, warning of retaliation for some recent transgression. Sometimes the message is close to literal: it could be the realistic imitation, complete with masks and grunts, of the animals needed for the hunt; more symbolically, it may involve high jumps that indicate the desire for the corn to grow tall; still less directly, it may consist of a continuous, monotonous treading of the earth to waken the spirits of the underworld—to what purpose they would apparently know without having to be told. Even at such ingenuous levels, dance meaning has been manifested in a variety of ways.

We know that the Greeks and Romans wanted their theatre dance to serve as a kind of language. Augustine claimed this as the source of its value, for he declared that merely graceful motion pleases only the senses, leaving the mind unaffected. However, when an actor dances, the rhythmic movement of his limbs gives delight "yet, since to the attentive spectators all his gestures are signs of things, the dance itself is called *reasonable* because it aptly signifies and exhibits something over and above the delights of the senses." By specifying the actor, Augustine assures us that a movement concept alone would not satisfy his demand for a reasonable art; rather, he finds the value of dance in its capacity to imitate character, thought, and feeling. The Renaissance looked for symbolic values, while the eighteenth century returned to the idea of dance as a kind of drama involving actions and passions, though with lurking digressions intimating that the delights of airs and graces might be even more important. In general practice, a single form predominated until a new reformer called for dance to return to its true function of imitation—or its true function as pure movement—depending on which appeared needed at the time. The present situation is more complex. Despite a trend toward abstraction, a multiplicity of choreographic approaches coexist, and we had better beware of asking any one of them for a kind of meaning more appropriate to another.

Nelson Goodman distinguishes two kinds of movement in dance. First, there are the more "traditional" actions, those of a denotative type that involve "versions of the descriptive gestures of daily life . . . or of ritual." Then there are those, seen especially in the "modern dance," which exemplify rather than denote. What they exemplify, Goodman explains, "are not standard or familiar activities, but rather rhythms and dynamic shapes [which] may reorganize experience, relating actions usually associated or distinguishing others not usually differentiated, thus enriching allusion or sharpening discrimination." Wisely, Goodman does not insist that dance is limited to one or the other of these two types exclusively, for—although he does not suggest a range of possibilities—these types may certainly be seen as the extremities of a scale encompassing degrees of reference of which not only individual movements but dance itself is capable.

Where in this scale can we place the Sugar Plum Fairy? Surely her highly stylized vocabulary provides little direct reference to the activities of our daily lives, or even to the lives of the residents of late nineteenth-century St. Petersburg. By stretching the term a bit we may see some resemblance to ritual in the strict symmetry, the clear-cut formal patterns, the apparent lack of personal spontaneity. But we would be at a loss to say what kind of ritual was being represented other than, perhaps, the ritual of a ballet dancer dancing. Still, though her individual movements seem to belong to the category that Goodman describes as exemplification of rhythms and dynamic shapes, the dance as a whole seems to refer to rather personal, if not very individual, qualities—graciousness, friendliness.

We are, in fact, faced with a rather lengthy continuum, from nearly realistic denotation to exemplification of forms. Generally, this has been the course of the historical evolution of western dance, though actually the development has been cumulative, because contemporary styles practically run the gamut, while previous periods appear to have been more homogeneous. Some descriptions of early works may look deceivingly nonrepresentational, as does Beaujoyeulx's account of the finale of his *Ballet Comique de la Reine* of 1581: In the last *entrée* "They danced the grand Ballet of forty passages or Geometric figures. These were exact and considered in their diameter, sometimes square, now round, and with many and diverse forms, and so often triangular, accompanied by some square and other small figures . . . everyone believed that Archimedes could not have better understood Geometric proportions." Certainly this sounds abstract but deceivingly so, for the assembled audience knew that the figures were symbolic of the mutation of the elements and the seasons, of moral choice and right direction, and the choreographer had no need to explain conventions that were so well understood by his contemporaries.

Thereafter, representation remained dominant but took various forms. The court ballet had its types of lovers, drunkards, and thieves who gave coherence to an otherwise episodic entertainment. The eighteenth century had its Greek gods and heroes; the romantic era its sylphs and longing lovers. Even the dances in divertissements had reference to a type of personality or a class—drunkards, bores, sailors, Scotsmen, fairies—so the choreographer always had some basic character motifs to work with. Dance as exemplification appeared later, though I would not urge, as Goodman does, that it is especially associated with the modern dance, partly because that term has become so ambiguous and partly because exemplification now dominates a considerable segment of the current ballet repertory.

How all these developments came about is a concern of the historian; what matters here is that today's audience has a rich store of varieties of dance at its disposal, and each provides a distinctive kind of experience. As we have just seen in the case of the Sugar Plum Fairy, looking for properties that are irrelevant to the type leads only to frustration. Furthermore, she is not a uniquely problematical instance. The range is extensive and the dividing lines are often elusive. Nevertheless, some fundamental categories might be worth distinguishing.

Yuri Grigorovich's *Ivan the Terrible* is not only based on an historic personage, but also portrays incidents drawn from events that are known to have occurred. These are minutely detailed; there are conspiracies and battles and celebrations and love scenes. Moments of dancing alternate with extended scenes of near-literal gesturing. The Soviet choreographer has stated that he selected from history those episodes that show how the Russian people withstood the terrors of the sixteenth century, but it is easier for most spectators to pity the poignant Anastasia or fear the treacherous boyars than to care very much about the anonymous crowd and the patriotic theme. Realistic sets and period costumes support the impression of specificity. This is denotation with a vengeance.

On the contrary, Martha Graham's treatment of Jocasta stresses universality. Isamu Noguchi's set for *Night Journey* is starkly symbolic; the use of a chorus, functioning much like the one in Greek tragedy, lifts the narrative to the sphere of ritual. The gestures of the chorus signify warning and then grief, they surge across the stage like a furious whip. Events are alluded to in phrases of evocative images rather than being depicted literally. The love duet, structured as a flashback and fractured by tensions of remembrance, represents no particular moment in time but portrays the convoluted life cycle—woman as lover and beloved, simultaneously wife and mother, serving the marriage bed and the cradle.

In Antony Tudor's *Dark Elegies* the situation is still more abstract. The singer tells of grief for the deaths of children, but he sings in German, which not everyone in the audience can understand. The dancers are a group of mourners, but otherwise we know nothing about them. Although there are solos and duets, no one appears as an individual. Together they present shapes of grief—now frantically rebelling against fate with arms slashing into the unmoved air; now helplessly overcome, the body curled up on itself. The conclusion is a scene of resignation and acceptance, though the reason for the change is not given and there is no dramatic turning point.

This brings us to the Sugar Plum Fairy, for in her case we cannot define a specific character or experience, nor can we even name an emotion. Still, a persona is revealed by movements that I once described as exhibiting qualities of behavior but that I would now prefer to designate more broadly as qualities of temperament.

I like even more Noël Carroll's adaptation of Heidegger's "ways of being-in-the-world", though it must be understood that the phrase is not used in Heidegger's very specific sense, but rather as a general mode of living, acting. Our fairy radiates an unaffected charm; she is ladylike, but not stuffy, quite an ideal hostess whose easy manner never suggests that she has spent the day slaving over her Cuisinart.

Next: Doris Humphrey described her *New Dance* as a work of affirmation, moving from disorganization to organization. In structure the dance passes from the simple to the complex, from an individual integration to a group integration. The final "Celebration" presents a harmonious chorus in which no member is more important than another. Though a kind of joyousness permeates the last section, the feeling is not the point. The evolving patterns of solos, duets, and trios, which emerge from and return to the constantly turning group, are significant not of feelings but of ideas of order: the orderly balance of elements within a whole, the orderly conduct of people in relation to one another that gives pleasure to both the individual and the society. Here, I believe, we have left representation behind and encountered our first instance of exemplification. The conclusion of *New Dance*—the ensemble holding to a steady 4/4 rhythm, the soloists dancing phrases of seven, seven, and ten, all ending together on the count of twenty-four—exemplifies the concept of a harmonious society. The "rhythms and dynamic shapes" are presented as a metaphor of a potential of human experience.

Balanchine also choreographs works that use movements to exemplify patterns, but he would prefer that they be enjoyed for their own sake, he does not want them considered as suggestive of anything else. To him a ballet is like a rose: you look at it and delight in it, but you don't ask what it means. Balanchine's explanation for the variety of forms his roses have taken is always the same: the music. The music tells him whether his movement should be expansive or constricted, flowing or percussive, symmetrical or asymmetrical; it determines, in brief, his choice of choreographic style. He may give his ballet a title, but this should not be taken too seriously. It has been argued that in *Jewels* Balanchine failed to create "a structural isomorph of non-movement properties of objects," but he had no interest in nonmovement properties. Balanchine's jewels are his beautifully moving dancers.

Edwin Denby declared that the subject of Balanchine's *Agon* was a contest, but then admitted that it had nothing to do with winning or losing. The subject, he noted, "is shown by an amusing identity in the action, which is classic dancing shifted into a 'character' style by a shift of accentuation. The shift appears, for example, in the timing of transitions between steps or within steps, the sweep of arm position, in the walk, in the funniness of feats of prowess. The general effect is an amusing deformation of classic shapes due to an unclassic drive or attack. . . . *Agon* shifts traditional actions to an off-balance balance on which they swiftly veer. But each move, large or small, is extended at top pitch. Nothing is retracted. The ardent exposure is that of a grace way out on a limb. . . . The emotion is that of scale." *Agon* exemplifies ideas of dancing with its speed and spaciousness, with its complexity and its power and its tenderness. It is movement quality made manifest.

So far, regardless of the degree of specificity involved, the meaning of the dance has been determinate: the person, feeling, or event represented, the idea or form exemplified, can be rather strictly defined. With Merce Cunningham, however, this is not the case: "I start with a step. . . . This is not beginning with an idea that concerns character or story, a fait accompli around which the actions are grouped for reference purposes. I start with a movement . . . then out of this the action begins to assume its own proportions, and other possibilities appear as the dance proceeds. New situations present themselves—between the dancers, the dancers and the space, the space and the time. It is not subject to a prearranged idea of how it should go." He added: "Each spectator may interpret the events in his own way."

The spectators are free to interpret—so says the choreographer. Is the range of possibilities unlimited? By his permissiveness, yes, but the reactions seldom range far from a fixed center, for in any Cunningham dance the type of movements clusters around a sort of syndrome of family resemblance. "I have a feeling," the choreographer told Clive Barnes, "that it produces some kind of atmosphere." Again the movements exemplify "rhythms and dynamic shapes," but their applicability in this case is to a distinctive mode of associating and distinguishing that is concerned with the dancer's awareness of his relation to time and space, to the varieties of qualities of energy he exerts on time and space. Carolyn Brown described it as "'shaking up' established or familiar ways of moving." Certainly an experience of enrichment, but quite different from that of *New Dance* or *Agon*.

Sharing some, but not all, aspects of Cunningham's approach are the new conceptual artists. Their choreography, too, exemplifies rhythms and patterns, but their emphasis is different. Cunningham's compositional devices serve as means to discovering unexplored ways in which human energy can be used in time and space. The system itself is not important to the audience; only the consequences of its use are significant. For the conceptual choreographers, however, the idea and the process of its realization are more important than the result. The meaning of the dance lies in the working out of the system. Program notes guide the viewer, as in these for Dana Reitz's *4 Scores for Trio*: The first score is concerned with "opening up movement possibility"; in the second the movements are "pressured with increasing speed, volume, space, force"; in the third each dancer makes solo experiments; finally "the first score is replayed and opened with new information . . . combinations, movements, rhythms, moments, intensities, relationships are changed."

The choreographers belonging to the group that Arlene Croce calls the "Mercists" have dominated much of contemporary American dance, but the last two decades have also witnessed a concurrent development in semirepresentational, dramatic forms. Meredith Monk is a leading exponent of a new kind of expressive theatre that is not literally referential but rather suggestive and symbolic, combining realistic objects and actions with bizarre images and fragmented structures. *Quarry*, for example, presents simultaneously—in various areas of the performing space—scenes of a sick child lying in bed, a group of young women at a dinner table, an actress rehearsing her lines, a scholar discussing his research, and an elderly couple who seem to belong to biblical times. The ensuing action concerns all of these characters, relating the sick child to the sick world of the Holocaust in sequences that adhere to no chronological or logical order but create a terrifying emotional impact.

Some choreographers of all these types have used written notes to tell the audience what was going on in their dances. So we have had sometimes complete librettos (on sale in the lobby) or more or less extensive summaries in the (free) house program to make sure that the plot of the ballet is clear. On occasion, relevant historical and biographical material is included. Though the position of the formalist choreographer is quite different, he too may alert observers with a few words suggesting that they look out for some particular movement themes and structures, since recognizing them will enhance their enjoyment of the dance. The conceptualist explains his system, but fundamentally, I think, most choreographers would like to have their meaning grasped directly, straight from the stage to the mind—or heart—of the audience. They have done some thinking about how to facilitate this process.

According to Doris Humphrey, the technique that turned ordinary gesture into dance was also the technique that enabled the choreographer to communicate most graphically with the viewer.

She observed that the change of any one element—such as the space, the tempo, the direction, the part of the body that moves—could give an ordinary action the look of dance by making it appear extraordinary. Further, the alteration increased the specificity of the portrayal. Watching her work out these variations, as I did one summer at Connecticut College, it was impossible to deny the effects she assigned to the deviations: people shaking hands while bending backward certainly did look like stuffed shirts; a phrase performed without a climax did indeed make the action appear wooden. But why? Her answer was simple: we make these associations from experience; the patterns, although exaggerated, are recognizable from life; these are patterns of everyday behavior made both more interesting and more manifest by stylization.

The dramatic choreographer is concerned not only that the audience recognize the identity of the characters represented, but also that they be moved by the feelings which are expressed by the characters. John Martin reasoned that we react kinesthetically; in imagination our bodies assume the shapes and rhythms and tensions that we see on the stage. These physical dispositions are familiar to us. We have experienced them before, and they remind us of the feelings that previously caused our own bodies to assume these identical shapes and rhythms and tensions. But Rudolf Arnheim argued that such factors as speed, shape, and direction do not alone arouse the viewer: "It is the kind of directed tension or 'movement'—its strength, place, and distribution—transmitted by the visible patterns that is perceived as expression." The perceptual elements of the dancer's movements are not simply recorded by the nervous system of the observer; rather, it is the dynamic quality produced by those elements that arouses the corresponding configuration of forces in him.

Of course these configurations must be familiar to us if we are to respond to them. The contours of the body as it experiences basic emotions are common to most human beings—the shapes of grief, joy, love, hate are recognizable the world over. The artist, however, makes us not only recognize the emotion but respond to it. The merely quantitative imitation of shapes is sufficient to convey the idea that the character is sad, that the dancer represents a sad person. But this may not bring about the expression of sadness that will generate a sympathetic response in the viewer. At this point, Humphrey's modes of stylization come into play, intensifying the dynamic qualities of strength or weakness, tension or release, that assure communication. Then the choreographer achieves what Arnheim called "the kind of stirring participation that distinguishes artistic experience from the detached acceptance of information."

In the case of dance especially, the experience need not be of a particular situation or character, for movement is better suited than words (though less well suited than music) to express generalized feeling. We do not question the exact nature of Martha Graham's grief in *Lamentation*; she is the sheer essence of sorrow. Still more abstractly, Ashton's *Symphonic Variations* reflects in its calm, sustained movement phrases, and in its balanced groupings, a microcosm of order and proportion. We do not ask who these people are or where on earth they exist.

Arnheim remarked that "motifs like rising and falling, dominance and submission, weakness and strength, harmony and discord, struggle and conformance, underlie all existence." While this comment comes from a discussion of art in general, it is interesting that so many of his terms may be read as relating to movement. Here we see again those qualities of temperament, those ways of being-in-the-world, that distinguish so much non-narrative dance. Cunningham would not exclude the possibility of their association with his choreography; they can be heard in the music that is visualized in the ballets of Balanchine; they can be found in the systems of the conceptualists; they assume mythical proportions in the work of Meredith Monk.

If these are qualities that underlie all existence, we should find them unfailingly recognizable. Yet new audiences frequently fail to understand, and without understanding they cannot be moved. What can keep movement from communicating?

Providing that the dance is not very well choreographed, we would have no problem finding the answer. The dramatic choreographer can fail to stylize his movements sufficiently or, through overelaboration, he may disguise the source gesture. Or both he and the formalist may be wronged by faulty execution on the part of the performer. Both again, but the formalist especially, may fail to provide a clear case; the movement may lack sufficient distinction or consistency so that unintended ambiguity results. Yet the aborted communication may not be due at all to the incompetence of the artists.

Much has been said in the field of semiotics about our need to understand the language in which a sign occurs in order to understand the sign. I especially like what Ladislav Matejka remarked about being "attuned" to the language of the artist if his sign structure is to function as a mediator between the work of art and its audience. Knowing the dictionary meaning is not enough, especially in the theatre where a sympathetic attitude—a willing suspension of disbelief—may be necessary as well. Our individual responses tend to be governed by an internalized system, Matejka noted; a system that has been established by the community, the culture in which we happen to find ourselves. Genetic inheritance and temperament are also factors. Consequently, some artistic systems will seem more congenial to us than others; in some cases we may have to exert a rather drastic effort if we are to make any sense of the signals, and even making sense of them will not guarantee our receiving pleasure.

The canon of classical ballet, as it existed in 1892, provided the language of *The Nutcracker*. Ivanov worked within what Joseph Margolis has called a relatively stable vocabulary, but established new relationships as he created within it. The basic movements were well known but they had never before been combined in quite this way—with this particular port de bras accompanying this sequence of steps, with the corps de ballet moving in this specific direction to exactly this goal position. The nature of the combinations was not startling, so they attracted no special attention. For the audience in the Maryinsky Theatre they spoke a familiar language. For today's adults it is a language somewhat familiar from memories of childhood lessons in manners and poise or from history books and pictures. Its meaning is remote but not inaccessible.

Yet the problem may be complicated. As Peter Kivy has remarked of music, expressiveness is bound first to conventions which govern the expression-behavior of a culture and second to artistic conventions which must be known to the audience that is to perceive the art of that culture with understanding and appreciation. Obviously, the dances of Africa and Asia pose even greater problems to westerners than *The Nutcracker*, which is at least a product of our own tradition. The values of nineteenth-century St. Petersburg's aristocratic society, and the theatrical formulas accepted as a matter of course by its members, do set up some barriers to communication, though lesser ones than those imposed by the conventions of still earlier eras. Shirley Wynne has described the ground rules for behavior in eighteenth-century France: "Practice moderation and forbearance, smile when in distress, remain articulate and calm." Translated into movement qualities these principles became: "Vertical (no elevation implied), narrow, and slender, with a general gathering in toward the vertical axis; the torso remained still, with a firm upright tension, while the head tilted and turned, and the shoulders shifted slightly in an epaulement. . . . The ballet retains the traditions of steps and patterns and the air of constraint that governed the performances of its ancestor."

But has it really retained them? Each era frames its own image of constraint, while new variations have been constantly added to the established steps and patterns, enriching the available ballet vocabulary. The pure style of the eighteenth century would probably look thin and monotonous to us now. At the time of Petipa and Ivanov tremendous changes had already occurred; the development of pointe work alone had added a new dimension to the character of classicism. The exhibition of virtuosity that thrilled the audience of *Swan Lake* would have offended a spectator at Versailles; Odette's eloquently arched back violated the firm upright of the minuet torso; shoulders and arms had grown progressively more fluid. In 1981 even these once innovative developments can pose problems for the unattuned viewer who now has considerably more advanced ideas about virtuosity and eloquence.

Yet time is not the exclusive creator of barriers. The problem recurs whenever an audience persists in bringing the same state of mind to any theatre, to any performance, arriving with expectations that are irrelevant to the situation and then proceeding to hold onto them. When Balanchine first took the New York City Ballet to London in 1950, he failed to provide the audience with their customary frame of reference, and many of them were lost without it. Richard Buckle summed up the attitude of the "crowd" in his "Critics' Sabbath":

> We want kings with haughty glance
> Wearing too much kit to dance;
> We want peasants in red breeches,
> We want puppy dogs and bitches;
> We want tunes like Piotr Ilyitch's,
> We want WITCHES, WITCHES, WITCHES! . . .
>
> We like psycho-sexo dramas,
> Tortured tarts in black pyjamas;
> We prefer a gesture lewd,
> To pirouettes en attitude. . . .

Something gay and something sad,
Orphans going to the bad,
Mr. Helpmann does it best,
Beaten up without his vest.
We want human interest . . .

Balanchine gave them another kind of interest; the syntax of classical dance. In each work, he endowed movement with a distinctive flavor, a particular rhythm and shape and energy that made *Concerto Barocco* flow coolly and serenely, while *Symphony in C* swept confidently through space, as *Four Temperaments* initiated some usually reticent movements with a sharp thrust, flattening others into "Egyptian"-type profiles, and contradicting the basic balletic curves with angled port de bras. It all required a sharp eye and an alert ear (the correlations with the music were significant), and a mind that did not insist on seeking a reference point outside the movement itself.

The 1950 Londoners should have read Denby's discussion of the kinds of ballet. Of the kind that uses stylized gesture he commented, "The pleasure of watching it lies in guessing the action it was derived from, in guessing what it originally looked like; and then in savoring the 'good taste' of the deformation." In the second kind the story is not very important and the enjoyment of the dancing itself is what the work is all about. Here the audience should watch differently: "It does not identify the gestures with reference to real life, it does not search in each pose for a distinct descriptive allusion. It watches the movements in sequence as a dance. . . . When the dance is over one understands it as a whole; one understands the quality of the dancer's activity, the quality of her rest, and in the play between the two lies the meaning of the dance aria." On another occasion he provided more detailed specifications, describing how the dancers "step out of one shape and into another, they change direction or speed, they erect and dissolve a configuration, and their secure and steady impetus keeps coming . . . one can respond to the visual significance . . . without being able to explain it reasonably."

As we begin almost romantically to see the dance as a symbol, as an embodiment of spiritual meaning, Denby reminds us of "the ease and fun and positive lightness" of ballet. Gently he insists on the need for a bit of pantomime in the course of an evening of classical dance. "It gives the feeling of being back in a more familiar rational world, back safe from the flight through the intuitive and rhythmic world of irrational symbols and of the charming animals."

If the meaning of the dance lies in the quality of the dancer's movement, the meaning of the *Nutcracker* variations does not go very deep. Nothing wrong with that. Most of us would find a diet of constant dance sublimity rather too rich for our tastes, and we do find it pleasant on occasion to be reminded of some of those vanished virtues, if not dating back to the minuet then at least to the age of social graces that produced the Sugar Plum Fairy. That world of irrational symbols and charming animals! True, it lacks relevance to our daily lives, but aren't we entitled to a little diversion? Or is it only diversion?

Surely *Swan Lake* offers more. It is involved with themes of good and evil, obedience and rebellion, fidelity, responsibility. There is a story, and most of the dances contribute to it—they establish situations, develop characterization, create suspense. Nevertheless, they often serve well in excess of their dramatic functions. The inward-focused movements of Odette's first solo speak of sorrow; her abruptly stopped sissonnes could express her thwarted efforts to escape. But we already know this about her, and so does Siegfried. Even realizing that information is not the point and therefore looking rather for intensification of emotional expression, we may find much of the choreography repetitive and dramatically superfluous. Is it at least appropriate?

The noble dignity of grace infuses the dancing of Odette; displays of strength would be out of place for her, though not for her rival. Odette is timid, Odile aggressive; the latter can be sexy, the former had better not. Through most of their first duet, Odette is supported by Siegfried; he holds her by the hand, by the waist, he rocks her in his arms. In the next act, Odile rushes assertively ahead of him, confidently assuming a pose before he catches up with her. Odette briefly raises her leg away from her body, then quickly, modestly, draws it back; Odile seductively prolongs the extension, simultaneously opening her arms, her physical self, to Siegfried.

Still, as we admire the dancing, momentarily caught up in its exquisite visualization of Tchaikovsky's melodies, we are having something more than a sensory experience, for the pathos of Odette and the effrontery of Odile have not been lost to us in the technical brilliance of the performance. The moods, though not specifically heightened in the course of the dances, are beautifully sustained. If the ballerina chooses, they may even be heightened as well, since there is room for interpretation. Within the scope allowed by the overall direction, some will decide to concentrate on the dramatic possibilities, making the dynamic contrasts more striking—using rubato to achieve a more languorous phrase or attacking a position with especially determined force. Others will select an approach that is less precise in its accent, more inclined to let the movement speak, however subtly, for itself. We may recall Denby's describing the dancers, stepping out of one shape into another . . . erecting and dissolving a configuration . . . the visual significance. . . . For significance it is. Arthur Symons saw the dancers "under the changing lights, so human, so remote, so desirable, so evasive . . . they seem to sum up in themselves the appeal of everything in the world that is passing and coloured and to be enjoyed."

Yuri Vladimirov and Natalia Besmertnova, as tsar and tsarina, fear the imminent treachery of the boyars in Yuri Grigorovich's *Ivan the Terrible*. *Photo by Mira.*

Bertram Ross and Martha Graham mourn the fate of all doomed lovers in her *Night Journey*. *Photo by Martha Swope.*

Terry Orr dances his grief against a background of depersonalized mourners in Antony Tudor's *Dark Elegies. Photo by Martha Swope.*

Doris Humphrey will return to the group after this solo in her *New Dance. Courtesy Dance Collection, The New York Public Library.*

In George Balanchine's *Agon,*
Allegra Kent and Arthur Mitchell
display a technical, rather
than an emotional relationship.
Photo by Martha Swope.

Meredith Monk is the sick child under the patchwork quilt in her *Quarry*; the world—
with a cloud-bearing procession and calisthenic exercises—goes on around her. *Photo by
Nathaniel Tileston.*

6. *Verbs of Motion*

"No, thanks. I *am* dancing."

Drawing by Saxon; © 1967
The New Yorker Magazine, Inc.

Perhaps the Russians dance so well because their language is so responsive to nuances of movement. From childhood they are made aware of, become sensitive to, the most subtle distinctions of motion, because their verbs are capable of extraordinary precision. With a bit of a prefix or the change of a vowel, a single word may mean: to set out, to go by, to approach, to get as far as, to arrive, to enter, to come upon, to drop in on, to make the rounds, to cross, to leave for a few minutes, to move away from something, to go away, to go too far—to say nothing of further slight variations which specify that the movement goes up or down or around, and there are different verbs to tell whether you do it in a vehicle or on foot and whether you do it every day or only once. The dancing master has no need for a string of adjectives that slowly explain the kind of movement he wants; he can quickly and exactly snap out his order. (He also has an advantage in counting: compare our flat "one" to his incisive, energetic "r-r-raz.")

Movement is the essence of dance. But the variations in ideas of how and how much dance has differed from ordinary movement, of what and how it has represented, expressed, or exemplified, should lead us to realize that works considered dances have been made of many kinds of movement and have used these kinds in many ways. Which is not to say that anything goes. Movement in dance (even if it lacks the grace and agility of "dance movement") is presented, framed, isolated from the world of practical motions that terminate with the attainment of a goal beyond themselves. What objects dance refers to, what properties it exemplifies, range from such specifics as Ivan the Terrible, through the ladylike graciousness of the Sugar Plum Fairy, to commentary on the modes of dancing itself. But dance is always about something, something that it displays, draws to our attention, not as a means to something else, but as an end in itself. It creates a world that exists apart from our real world, yet resembles it enough that perceiving the dance world can illuminate the real one. The glory of dance is that it has found so many ways to make us freshly conscious of all in the world that is "passing and coloured and to be enjoyed."

Most philosophers who have discussed dance do so on a level of generalities, which is only proper since their job is to deal with theories of art. As a pragmatist, however, I cannot help wishing they would go further, though often it is hard to see how their ideas could be applied to specific dance events. Of modern philosophers who have given serious attention to dance, Susanne Langer has written most extensively. Her theory of dance as the dynamic image has, quite rightly, attracted wide attention, for her ideas are of the greatest interest. Yet the possibility of their application remains problematic. Certainly Langer is correct in her claim that dance does not create its physical materials—bodies, space, gravity—but uses them "to create something over and above what is physically there: the dance . . . it springs from what the dancers do, yet it is something else." However, she continues with a more questionable assertion: "In watching a dance, you do not see what is physically before you—people running around or twisting their bodies; what you see is a display of interacting forces by which the dance seems to be lifted, driven, drawn, closed, or attenuated. . . . The physical realities are given. . . . But in the dance, they disappear; the more perfect the dance, the less we see of actualities."

I maintain that we *do* see what is before us even though the effect of the dance, when it succeeds, projects an energy, an ambience, a significance that is more than the sum of the events we observe occurring in time and space. We do not, to be sure, see the workings of the muscles of the dancers nor (we hope) hear their accelerated breathing or their heartbeats. But we do see their bodies and their actions, we see the shapes they make in relation to space and to one another, and we perceive their motions in time. For it is in virtue of their sensible properties that dances are distinctive. Langer argues that a work of art is a composition of "tensions and resolutions, balance and unbalance, rhythmic coherence, a precarious yet continuous unity. . . . Life is a natural process of such tensions, balances, rhythms; it is these that we feel in quietness or emotion as the pulse of our own living . . . [a dance is] an expression of its composer's knowledge of many feelings." Yet various dances express various feelings, and Langer's theory leaves us with no way to distinguish among kinds of dances, to account for the differences in our reactions to the dances we see.

To thrill us with feats of virtuosity, to strike us with pity and terror for a being whose body is tensed with struggle, to fascinate us by intricate coordinations punctuated by complex rhythmic accents, to move us by the simplicity and the wonder of a human being walking beautifully—these are some of the gifts of the diversity of dance. Langer does not want us to see "gymnastics and arrangements." If this signifies awareness of the means of the dance exclusively, if it means measuring the height of an arabesque or counting the fouettés, I would agree. But if it means ignoring the perceptible properties of dance, then it demands our forgoing the sensuous impressions that bid us fly with the virtuoso or weep with the wronged heroine. Langer has faulted dance writers who "play so freely across the line between physical fact and artistic significance." But when dance succeeds, that line disappears; the act and its significance are inseparable.

Maxine Sheets-Johnstone does draw distinctions. She separates dance that consists of "movement as sheer visual appearance" from the dance of "qualitative presence. . . . Both create a wholly qualitative world, but in the one quality appears in the guise of a moving form, and in the other as sheer pulsating energy." Again, the favored situation seems to involve the virtual disappearance of physical entities: "quality and quality alone shines forth." The author designates specific qualitative possibilities: "lyrical, bouncy, light, languid, fleet, powerful." Lyrical quality, for example, "creates a yielding space, there is nothing that opposes the flow of movement," which is "continuous, unbroken by jagged lines or directional sharpness." The time too is "an unbroken continuum." *Les Sylphides* fits this description nicely, but so do the very different dances in the style of Isadora Duncan—the former ethereal, the latter earthy. The Sheets-Johnstone account does not fit Taylor's *Aureole*, which makes use of both jagged lines and directional sharpness, though "lyrical" is surely the word that comes most readily to mind in recalling *Aureole*. When specifics are considered, the matter is seen to be far more complicated than this writer would lead us to believe.

Many factors have accounted for the range of styles visible in today's repertory; each choreographer has had to cope with limitations—ethical, psychological, physical, financial—imposed by his time and place of work. Each has functioned with a set of constraints more stringent than those existing for workers in any other art, for the motions of the human body, his instrument, are by its nature irrevocably limited. It is not like setting out to make a new musical instrument from inanimate materials. The individual choreographer also is limited by what his dancers have been trained to do—augmented by that little extra spark, whether ignited by his inspiration or their own vanity—that makes them go just so much farther than dancers have ever gone before. Yet gravity is still with us in the world, and humans will forever lack the loose-knit structure that makes the cat so marvelously flexible.

As if these constraints were not enough, Paul Taylor has reminded us of some other problems with dancers: "They have character and personality, which they ASSERT. They have individual traits, and just when you think you know how to handle them they CHANGE. Not like canvas that stays stretched once and for all."

The natural constraints of the medium also limit the range of subjects that can be represented by dance, providing the choreographer wants to represent. Balanchine's famous statement that it is impossible to portray mothers-in-law in dance does seem irrefutable. True, Agnes de Mille managed to convey the idea of stepmother without words in *Fall River Legend*: the father places a white shawl, already associated with the mother who has died, around the shoulders of another woman while his daughter watches. Presto: stepmother. But that is not using a movement to describe the character; it is using a visual device, which is theatrically fair enough, but it is not relying on dance. Choreographers keep trying. I watched Valery Panov's version of Dostoevsky's *The Idiot* carefully to see how he would handle the moment described in the program as "Aglaja calls Natasya a whore." I missed it.

Nineteenth-century ballet solved the problem with conventional mime, some of it based on recognizable social gestures (for example, arms spread in welcome), some of it rather remote (an arm circling the face to signify beauty). Either the audience knew the code or they didn't care—more likely the latter. These devices are now out of fashion, partly because we have become more demanding of expressive movement but partly also because we have become accustomed to another kind of theatrical pacing. We will accept some slow mime in a repertory piece, but our expectations warn the choreographer not to try it in a new one.

Some modern choreographers have chosen a very different approach, which has produced at least two dramatic dance masterpieces. Both Limón's *The Moor's Pavane* and Ashton's *A Month in the Country* are based on plots that seem hopelessly inappropriate to telling by means of movement—Shakespeare's *Othello* is full of complicated intrigues, while Turgenev's play contains numerous discussions but little action. Both work in dance because each choreographer has taken from his source only those scenes that center on emotional climaxes. Limón uses the handkerchief scheme and just four characters whose violent passions are framed by the cold formality of a court dance. Ashton structures his ballet on a series of duets that exhibit personal relationships that inevitably lead to a romantic crisis. Neither tries to rival the drama. They do what dance can do—beautifully.

The choreographer must work within the constraints imposed by his medium. He confronts other restrictions as well: the space of the stage, the technical equipment of the theatre, the current expectations of his audience. And of course there is always a limit on the amount of money available. Yet with all their constraints, choreographers have created such a range of verbs of motion as the Russian grammarians never dreamed of.

To be sure, the choreographer's work is not only a matter of coping with constraints. He is also offered very positive resources from which to choose. While the changing products of time and place impose constraints, they also offer him fresh possibilities. Some eras offer a broader range than others; this has been especially true in the area of techniques. The situation has not been purely cumulative, because some parts of traditional vocabularies have been discarded and lost with time. Still, the general tendency has been toward the expansion of possibilities. New ideas become important in the world; new subject areas become permissible for treatment in the theatre (Freudian themes alone have opened a tremendous territory). New theories of organization appear in the artistic environment: composing by chance, by tasks, in accordance with any number of conceptual devices that free the choreographer from the demands of dramatic representation. Insofar as he selects from materials that are currently available, the choreographer reflects the world in which he lives.

Inevitably, the resulting selections tend to form clusters marking off those works that seem to exhibit similar characteristics, which we then distinguish as styles. Although the primary element involved with stylistic distinctions in dance is, and should be, the nature of the movements performed by the dancers, another set of factors tends to enter in—types of plot, relative importance of decor and costumes, kind of staging, among the most obvious.

But even when writers pay lip service to these various components, discussions of styles of dance have often been grossly oversimplified. We had romantic ballet in the early nineteenth century and classical ballet in the later nineteenth century. What we had in the seventeenth and eighteenth centuries was called ballet then, though some now try to view it as a kind of "preballet," thus avoiding the curious situation of having a classic style both precede and follow a romantic one.

In the twentieth century we have had ballet and modern dance. The latter, once conceived as applying to almost anything that was not ballet, has been given a reprieve by being divided into modern and postmodern, while Cunningham, who belongs chronologically between the two, seems to be left in limbo as belonging to neither (though the art historians would have saved him with the designation of "late modern"). Now, however, the postmodern label, which originally covered the aesthetic of the Judson Dance Theatre and its followers of the 1960s, is applied to a most heterogeneous assemblage of choreographers, who sometimes seem to have only the label in common.

The easy way to see contemporary dance is in terms of broad categories: ballet, modern, and (often with a slight sneer) Broadway-musical-type dance. This frequently used division has caused considerable distortion and confusion, raising my favorite question of recent years: "Where do we put Twyla Tharp?" Attempts at more specific formulations have not always succeeded either; an example is the designation of "multimedia artist." This certainly applies to Alwin Nikolais, whose works of movement, sound, shape, and color utilize electronic sound devices, films, slide projections, a varied assortment of stage properties (such as masks, screens, ropes), and dancers. Often he was accused of "dehumanizing" by making the dancer only one part of his total theatre concept. But that is one accusation which has not been hurled at Meredith Monk, who is also called a multimedia person and who uses such devices. The Nikolais pieces steer clear of drama; they have no plot, no literal characters, no recognizable mood; they are kinetic designs for the eye and the ear. Nikolais invites us to marvel rather than feel. But Monk makes us feel. Her use of media serves her symbolic system of archetypal images. A film of people stumbling through a rock quarry, of archeologists at their digs; a girl in a big hat, the sound of a train whistle—each appears first as an intriguing but mysterious object, then develops into a metaphor. There are images of seeking and discovering, and always of travel, of journeys to the future that are also excursions into the past. Both choreographers use multimedia, but that is only one of their choices; others are equally or more important, and we need to look closely at all of them.

Provided by his society and by his artistic environment with both constraints and possibilities, the choreographer is bound to reflect the state of contemporary culture. But if he must put up with his constraints, albeit with some minor rebellions, he does not have to—and in fact cannot—accept all the possibilities open to him. Although in *Deuce Coupe* Tharp managed to have her central figure go through the better part of the ballet alphabet from "ailes de pigeon" to "voyagé," the choreographer usually has to select from the possibilities according to the way he wants to define the character, set the mood, or exhibit the movement theme. Natalia Makarova has suggested that style may come from "a knowledge of what must *not* be done . . . it is a particular system of restrictions concerning the positions of arms, hands, feet, chest, shoulders, and head. If we stop observing these restrictions, all ballets will look alike." Of course, much more than the positions of body parts are involved—rhythm, dynamics, use of space, and many other factors enter into the picture—but Makarova is right about the restrictions. Speaking as a choreographer, Paul Taylor agrees. After starting with a mind open to possibilities, he feels that "the really helpful part is the restrictions. You decide what not to do."

From materials provided by reality, the choreographer makes

choices that impose a form of stylization on reality: only certain objects are selected for representation; only certain feelings, certain qualities of character, are expressed; only certain modes of moving are exemplified. The balance of the real world—with its myriad beings and artifacts, its multiple modes of feeling and behaving, its many manners of moving—is systematically excluded. In this way the artist stylizes his real material, points up what he considers important, focuses the attention of the audience where he wants it. The sensibility of the choreographer reveals itself through his choices, through his deliberate system of restrictions, which may eliminate from a particular vocabulary, or from a broad palette of movement potential, all but what he wants his audience to perceive. His comment comes to us through his style.

In his discussion of classical music, Charles Rosen sees a great style as a synthesis of the artistic possibilities of an age; the irrelevant residue of previous traditions is discarded, the relevant elements work together with coherence, power, and richness. Rosen's theory stresses the role of complexity; he is concerned with the ease or tension with which a language is used, noting that when facility takes over, the style really ceases to be a forceful system of communication. If coherence is easily achieved, if there is small threat to unity, there is little to excite us. We may add the possibility that the system has become too familiar; it has lost its cogency. What is easy, familiar, is taken for granted; it no longer moves our consciousness to alert attentiveness. (We are reminded of Graham's hidden realities behind the accepted symbols.) A simple, familiar language fills a simple, common need; great art answers to our most profound questions, even—perhaps especially—the ones that we cannot formulate in words.

Great art—and dance is no exception—tends to be difficult, yet its admirers find the required effort worthwhile. Nelson Goodman has noted that "an obvious style, easily identified by some superficial quirk, is properly decried as a mere mannerism. A complex and subtle style, like a trenchant metaphor, resists reduction to a literal formula. . . . The less accessible a style is to our approach and the more adjustment we are forced to make, the more insight we gain and the more our powers of discovery are developed."

But caution is necessary here. Ballet and modern dance have often been considered styles, the former simple and the latter complex (or vice versa). They are not styles at all in Goodman's sense of the term, which refers to properties manifested by a work that are characteristic of an author, period, region, or school. Rather, they are genres, broader categories or types that may encompass a number of styles, any of which may then be found simple or complex. Once such styles have been defined, we must still beware of the possibility of borrowings among them and even of the potentiality of a style taking on some of the properties previously linked exclusively to a genre other than the one with which it is usually associated. This does not necessarily result in a "merging" of the genres; that would occur only if their respective qualities should exist in the new work in such an ambiguous balance that they negate one another. Any real genre is usually characterized by the presence of more than a single quality, though conceivably some one quality may be discovered to be its sine qua non, while others may be somewhat modified without endangering the identity of the type. Perhaps the time has come for a test.

Ballet seems the logical place to start because on the surface it is so clearly accessible; we start children with ballet before we take them to operas or symphony concerts. T. S. Eliot was aware of a paradox: "The ballet is valuable because it has, unconsciously, concerned itself with a permanent form; it is futile because it has concerned itself with the ephemeral in content." He found it "a liturgy of very wide adaptability" that had not been used to its full potential. But we may take his clue and look for the form that underlies the obvious specifics.

By "ballet" let us say we mean what is usually considered its quintessential style, classical, if by "classical" we mean pure. Lincoln Kirstein once defined style as a moral virtue manifested in the conquest of untidy egotism; ballet as "a clear if complex blending of human anatomy, solid geometry and acrobatics, offered as a symbolic demonstration of manners." To John Martin it was "a glorification of the person as person, the presentation of its ideal essence freed from the encumbrances of a rationalistic universe of cause and effect." Adrian Stokes suggested deftness and economy or neatness; Edwin Denby cited lightness, elevation, and ease. Kirstein qualified: "clean and open, grandiose without affectation, noble without pretension." All of which sounds suspiciously like our old friend grace. But we should try to be more specific.

The answer is simple, of course; we have known for many years that classical style is movement based on the five positions of the feet. But we are looking for the principle that is manifested in the five positions, and that is the principle of outwardness, of *en dehors*. Generally this term refers to the rotation of the legs in the hip socket, popularly known as "the turnout," and it is logical to consider this first, not only because it accounts for those five positions, but because it constitutes the major physical task to be accomplished by the ballet student. Without the rotation a great part of the classical vocabulary is out of reach, its major feats—shoulder-high extensions that do not disturb the equilibrium, multiple pirouettes, intricate entrechats—are difficult if not impossible to execute.

If this outwardness were limited to the legs, however, the body as a whole would look incongruous. In the full classical style, the entire person appears in extroversion—open to other bodies, open to the surrounding space. But not vulnerable, because the rib cage is held erect, confidently; the arms seem buoyantly lifted away from the body, the head appears to float atop a long, vertical, relaxed spine.

Outwardness is not practical for the affairs of everyday life. It does not facilitate progress in a direct, forward line, as in running to catch a bus; it makes the body occupy more space, which is inconvenient in a crowded elevator. Yet it is quite reasonable for a style that developed in a royal court, where to move in an ordinary manner would have been considered demeaning. The idea was to look noble, gracious, rather than serviceable. The en dehors facilitates useless actions; it creates a state of dancing. The classical ballet style—brilliant and elegant—does not exist without it.

Yet the en dehors, while it is essential to classical ballet, is not unique to it. Outwardness also characterizes India's Bharata Natya, where the legs are fully turned out and the torso is held high as in ballet, but contrary to ballet the dancer remains almost constantly in demi-plié, her whole foot on the floor, often stamping into the floor. The acknowledgment of weight in the lower body seems to contradict another classical balletic quality, which is a prevalent upward thrust. For Volynsky, "with the vertical begins the history of human culture and the gradual conquest of heaven and earth." The ballerina raises herself to greet the gods. The Hindu view is different; its gods come down to visit mortals.

In classical ballet if the supporting knee is bent, it is usually only as a preparation for a rising movement. Most often the entire body is stretched; the variety and range of jumps are tremendous, and jumps are often extended by lifts. Pointe work, a natural extension of the upward thrust, was originally developed to enhance the portrayal of the ethereal sylph, but—like the aristocratic association of the turnout—the connotation is dispensable. Length of line and brilliance are enhanced by the use of pointes. Yet we can recognize classical style even when there are no jumps or lifts and no pointe work. We would not recognize it, though, if it failed to exhibit that sense of upward reaching, if it failed to stress verticality, which Volynsky called the line of exultation.

Lightness, so frequently considered an attribute of classical style, is often associated with verticality, with reason, since it relates to the height of the placement of the center of gravity in the body.

It was essential for the fairy creatures of the romantic ballet and to some other character types in dramatic works (the slippery Younger Sister in *Pillar of Fire* is an example). There are also more abstract contexts where allegro movement is exploited for its own sake, and the impression of speed is enhanced—and also made physically possible—by the accompanying lightness of the body, the feet seeming to flutter in the air (as Merrill Ashley's do in Balanchine's *Square Dance*).

Male dancers, including those who excel in elevation, seldom produce an appearance of sheer lightness, for the man more often stresses vigor with a firmness of stance and tread that show him to be in command of the situation. Yet we do not find him un-balletic; he is not a stevedore type. The attack is strong but not heavy. Further, it never intrudes on, never distorts, the clean line of the movement. Actually, the emphasis was not always quite so far on the side of strength. Bournonville, in the mid-nineteenth century, included among his virtues as a dancer a manly joie de vivre. Today the Bournonville jump, a model of elasticity and lightness, stands as a charming souvenir of another era. Nowadays even the woman does not always want to exhibit lightness. Sometimes the reason is dramatic—as in the case of the vicious females who exult in their prowess in Jerome Robbins's *The Cage*—but sometimes it is simply a matter of desired movement quality—as the opening of the Balanchine/Stravinsky *Symphony in Three Movements*, where even the girls' long flowing hair accentuates their sensuous weightedness.

Is virtuosity necessary? That may be going too far; skilled movement might be sufficient if by virtuosity we mean the all-out, knock-'em-dead kind. Nor need ballets be works of virtuosity, exhibiting the skills that are their subject matter. But evidence of skill, of control beyond the ordinary, must, I think, be visible in the performance. André Levinson wrote that "the very illusion of this enchanting art—which seems to ignore all natural laws—depends on an intelligent ordering of physical effort. The [classical] dancer then is a body moving in space according to any desired rhythm." That intelligent ordering, manifested in every move, signifies the dancer's mastery; it creates the illusion that he is exempt from the restrictions of natural laws. Such laws account for the basic incompetence of the untrained body; it is seldom capable of maintaining an exact rhythm or following a completely straight line or moving in exact coordination with a group. All dancers have to do these things, but classical style demands them more stringently. It evokes Valéry's idea of another state of existence.

An additional quality that has been assigned to classical style is clarity. No extraneous actions detract our attention from the shape the dancer wants us to see, from the rhythm he wants us to feel. Frequently, this entails movement that is goal-oriented: reaching the exact point in space at the exact point in time is important; the resulting shape is frequently held for a while so that it can be fully enjoyed. This does not mean that movements have to be simple; they may be extraordinarily complicated, full of intricacies and surprises (the Bournonville dancer bounces along a circular path to the left and suddenly reverses direction in a diagonally directed grand jeté). The richest styles have a clarity that is not immediately perceivable, which is true in all the arts but is especially challenging in dance, because—until video discs become common property—we cannot keep looking back at the work to discover the structural secret that illuminates it all. Still, an underlying kinetic logic tends to make itself felt, even when it resists conscious definition.

Clarity is relevant, not only to the movements of an individual dancer, but to the configurations of an ensemble as well. Balanchine's *Le Tombeau de Couperin* depends for much of its effectiveness on the dancers' precision in maintaining a series of intricate designs of lines and semicircles and waving paths. The Rockettes present a similar case of reliance on accurate formations, which means that we have another instance in which a property is essential, but not unique, to ballet.

Concomitant to clarity is the self-revealing nature of classical style; it may, of course, reveal something beyond itself (though some theorists wish that it would not), but it always calls attention to its kinetic qualities; the ballerina's eye follows her flowing arm or looks down at her nimble feet; the man admires his partner's pirouettes or extends the line of her arabesque with his arms. Movement is displayed. Sometimes what is displayed is fantastic virtuosity, but not always. Balanchine's dancers sometimes, as in *Chaconne*, just walk—simply, and not at all simply, they walk. How beautiful a walk can be when it is not trying to get somewhere! Luminous, Volynsky would call it. Valéry said of the dancer (who was surely a ballet dancer) that "she teaches us that which we do, showing clearly to our souls that which our bodies accomplish obscurely." This seems essential to the classical style.

One more factor may be considered. "A machine for manufacturing beauty," said André Levinson of the ballet dancer, provoking a good deal of indignation from those who wanted to preserve her humanity. But Levinson was not alone in his conviction that the discipline undergone by the performer resulted in her forgoing a natural method of functioning in order to take on an aesthetic mode: "To discipline the body to this ideal function, to make a dancer of a graceful child, it is necessary to begin by dehumanizing him, or rather by overcoming the habits of ordinary life. . . . The accomplished dancer is an artificial being, an instrument of precision." Most theorists, disliking the term "dehumanize," prefer "impersonal," but I suspect they mean approximately the same thing. Martin spoke of an "ideal essence." That the exercises of the ballet dancer have been likened to ritual is no accident. Kirstein recalls Colette's Cheri, taunting his icy wife: "It's as if I'd married a ballet-dancer. Nine o'clock sharp, the Class: it's sacrosanct." Or Violette Verdy commenting on

Rudolf Nureyev and the first position: "It's like the Sign of the Cross everyday." It is curiously reminiscent of that other dance form characterized by en dehors: Bharata Natya was designed for use in the temple. Such techniques mold the dancer to conform to the image—long, lithe, and with hidden strength—regardless of his real personality. The dancer always appears as a persona.

These qualities the classical dancer embodies with grace. Grace makes steps appear effortless, and—as if to prove that these incredible turns and extensions are really no trouble at all—grace connects them in a seamless flow, with no stops for determined preparations, and throws in a few broderies for good measure. Any sign of the practical, of the merely utilitarian, is forbidden. The classical style may be the highest manifestation we know of the image of grace.

If we look closely at all these properties, no one appears to be sufficient in itself to qualify the style as classical ballet, and no one is unique to this style. Nevertheless, their combination does create something unique. How many of them must be present and in what proportion should, I believe, be left unspecified. Why restrict possibilities? Apart from en dehors which, I suspect, must dominate any manifestation of classicism, the other qualities can, and certainly have, fluctuated considerably in the extent of their pervasiveness. I would hesitate, however, to term any of them completely optional, and I have not listed them (again excepting en dehors) in an order that I consider indicative of their relative importance. In fact, the degree of importance assumed by any of them might be taken as a key to the definition of a ballet style.

A choreographer who wants to work within the classical style accepts these constraints, which still offer him a considerable number of choices regarding relative emphasis. Many areas of choreographic choice remain free, undefined. Classical rhythms tend to be regular but are not necessarily so. Unison movement and symmetry tend to characterize ensembles, though any balanced and ordered arrangement would be consistent with the other elements of the style. The nature of some works makes them more demanding of such uniformity. Some of our younger critics, observing the Bournonville festival in Copenhagen in 1979, found that they tired of poses that were always repeated or reversed symmetrically; it was all so predictable. But for Bournonville dancing is joy, and joy means that life is in harmony with nature and society; it is symmetrical. The balletic genre can take on a number of different qualities without violating its essential nature, but not an unlimited number of different qualities.

As yet nothing has been said about the ballet vocabulary, that codified collection of steps with French names that many little girls and some little boys learn after school. Appropriately performed the vocabulary displays the qualities of classical style. But style is a matter of structure and quality that can be manifested without the use of particular steps—though not without the use of particular kinds of steps. On the other hand, the steps can be performed in the terms of other styles. There is nothing irrevocably balletic about failli-assemblé, as Humphrey proved in her Bach *Partita*, where it is performed with the stress on landing into the floor instead of rising from it.

Which brings us to the question of "modern dance." An easy way out is to say that it lacks the balletic qualities; but so do many other forms of dance—tap, for example, and hula. Furthermore, some works labeled modern dance exhibit some of the qualities we have just assigned to ballet.

The latter was not always true, for the genre was founded at the time of World War I in a spirit of revolt. Mary Wigman stated her position: "Mannered and stilted [the ballet] could never tell what I had to say, which was purely personal." Miriam Winslow elaborated, defining the enemy form as "an attitude of impersonal presentation of movements designed by other persons to express beauty and truth (emotions and ideas) with the object of pleasing the onlookers." Modern dance, on the contrary, made the individual the center; it was "based upon the dancer's relationship to time and space, to life itself." The object was not to please, but to provoke and enlighten.

If modern dance is so truly personal, then it is bound to be heterogeneous. Can we find any common qualities? It depends on where we look.

For Humphrey it was "moving from the inside out"; for Graham it was "visualizing the interior landscape." Martin called it "the materializing of inner experience." Clear enough—for the 1930s and 1940s. In the 1950s Cunningham came along to negate the very core of identity claimed by his immediate predecessors. He denied that dance was about personal experience; it was, rather, about movement in time and space. Then came the defection of Judson group, who agreed with Cunningham's disdain of representation but added their own rejection of skilled movement. The fragmentation accelerated: conceptual dance, multimedia productions, a return to Graham's archetypal images but without her narrative structures, a return to Humphrey's lyricism but with even, balletic flow replacing her irregular breath rhythms. All these have been called modern dance.

What is modern dance? When I first worked on this problem of genres I read a paper on the subject at a conference where I first, rather neatly, defined ballet. When the moment came to do the same for modern dance, I was happily able to say that my time was up. Now, I fear, my time has come.

Kirstein defined modern dance as "a loose idiom of idiosyncratic, free-form movement, identified with careers and contributions of half a dozen individuals, all in their prime in 1935." Limón, who had just begun to choreograph in 1935 and who considered himself a modern dancer, wrote in 1966 that the modern dance is "a state of mind, a cognizance of the necessity of the art of the dance to come to terms with our time." But "free-form movement" is too vague to be useful, and Robbins's *Age of Anxiety* (1950), an exploration of the insecurity of the individual in contemporary society, certainly endeavored to cope with "our time" though it was called ballet.

Let us go back to movement. Watching ballet dancer Paolo Bortoluzzi in Limón's *The Moor's Pavane*, Anna Kisselgoff commented that the performance "was very much like kicking a football on a baseball diamond." She attributed the stylistic failure to lack of both proper technical training and conviction in the ideology that sparked the birth of the modern dance. Graham told Kisselgoff that the nature of the problem was indeed twofold: the ballet dancer lacked the necessary state of mind, but also tended to "learn by line instead of volume." Paul Taylor also suggested the latter kind of problem: "Ballet dancers are trained to concentrate on making shapes, rather than on what produced the shape." Laura Dean remarked that she is concerned about "not what the body does, but where the energy goes, with what quality it goes." Erik Bruhn had also essayed *The Moor's Pavane* but drew a somewhat different conclusion about the kind of adjustment he had to make to meet the requirements of a modern dance role: "It's a question of manipulating your weight. As the movements are generally earthbound, you have to find a different 'center.' You have to feel downwards, without looking as if you are digging into the ground."

Effort as opposed to the ballet dancer's ease? That may be part of it, but more broadly it might be viewed—and this is what some of the early moderns preferred—as an admission of humanity. Unlike the depersonalized ballerina—her struggles in the classroom stored away so that only the happy results are seen—the modern dancer reveals the process behind the movement. Limón used to speak of the drama of the modern dancer's jump. The ballet dancer soared without apparent effort—lovely! But how much more moving was the sight of a man, heavy and tense, raising himself, with willful determination, into the realm of the spirit.

Further possibilities have been suggested, the most common of them, perhaps, the negation of en dehors, the stress on turning inward, of the body folding in on itself. But insistence on this inwardness would eliminate most of the happier moments of the modern dance—Graham's ecstatic *Diversion of Angels*, for example, where a contraction sometimes leads not to an agonized closing but to a rapturous extension of body and limbs into aerial space. Senta Driver has suggested the addition of off-balance movements, twisting, and spiraling as elements much used by the modern dance. She does not, however, urge that these be considered essential to modern dance; only that they are characteristics sometimes found in modern dance and hardly ever found in ballet.

In movement we seem to find a broadening of the scope of the acceptable palette, a kind of permissiveness that in turn allows a greater range of qualities of being represented, of feelings expressed. Limón spoke with grandeur of saints and demons; now, Trisha Brown matter-of-factly tells the audience how she went on composing the dance as she performs it. Perhaps this is not a single genre . . .

If we do want to try to find a continuum, we must remember that any rigid formulation would contradict the outlook of the founders of the modern dance and immediately eliminate them as proper exhibitors of its qualities. We must also resist the temptation to make modern dance simply counter the properties of classicism, point by point. After all, ballet has been around for more than three hundred years, and the full extent of the qualities by which it is now known evolved only gradually. The earliest date usually set for the modern dance is the beginning of the twentieth century, when Duncan with her natural movement and Denishawn with its exoticism broke with the forms of conventional ballet. Some, however, would trace the origin of the genre that we now recognize back no further than the expressionism of Graham and Humphrey that emerged in the late 1920s. Around 1950 the nature of the modern dance changed radically with the advent of the chance techniques of Cunningham, and again a decade later with the ordinary movement presentations of the Judson group, and yet again with the appearance of such symbolist choreographers as Meredith Monk and Kenneth King. Today even the "postmodern" designation is risky, since we seem already to have a second generation of innovators, many of whom have adopted some of the qualities associated with the Rainer aesthetic but rejected others. Sally Banes suggests that the new virtuosity is nonillusionistic, "the gulf between artist and spectator has been irrevocably bridged." But I would not dare claim that anything about the modern dance is irrevocable; the future may hold many surprises. Meanwhile we have a past and a present diverse and rich enough to occupy our minds for quite some time. Can we identify the modern dance as a single entity?

If we cannot define a core, perhaps we can distinguish some outer limits, and we might try to do this in terms of tendencies that veer more in one direction than another. Generally, these tendencies might be viewed as an emphasis on path rather than goal in space; on weight rather than lightness in the body; on sharpness of accent rather than flow; on asymmetrical rather than balanced design; on exposure rather than concealment of process. But the situation has evolved with the years. The use of weight was far more important to the expressive phase of the modern dance than it is to the more formal styles of today. The exponents of everyday movement continue to stress weight, but for non-dramatic reasons: they want to call attention to the shapes of the ordinary. Taylor often combines weight with a flow that seldom stops at a defined position in space; Tharp juxtaposes weight and agility. Percussive accent and asymmetry have been submerged in Dean's repetitive spinning of matched figures, but she maintains the sense of weight and concern for path. We have various species of modern dance.

We also have modern ballet, a style that Deborah Jowitt once described as prettier than early modern dance but less polite than early ballet. However, she wrote this around 1970, when the prevalent type consisted of a basically classical vocabulary attacked with some of the qualities associated with modern dance, especially weight and sharpness. The altered dynamic was frequently justified by dramatic content, for early modern ballet took after early modern dance in its concern for expressiveness, though its themes tended to be less cosmic.

By 1980, however, modern ballet was something else again. Jennifer Dunning defined the school of Glen Tetley, Jiri Kylian, and Choo San Goh as "fast-paced, streamlined exercises in perpetual motion." The new style uses balletic turnout but scorns its traditional lightness for aggressive rather than delicate speed. Virtuosity, which was often highlighted at climactic points by the classical style, is now pervasive, thrilling chiefly by its accumulations—more dancers leaping higher and faster and stronger until the momentum wears itself out. Volynsky's exultation is replaced by exhaustion. Calling this a hybrid form clarifies nothing; it is a style of its own.

We are also developing a new kind of company, one that performs works drawn from the repertories of both ballet and modern dance choreographers. And why not? A symphony orchestra does not limit itself to playing a single musical genre. But in dance such diversity has seldom worked. Bodies trained in one manner of moving find it difficult to break long-standing habits. Also it seems that the cultivation of physical habits engenders psychological attitudes as well. This was most apparent in the early days of the modern dance when a real dichotomy existed: the ballet dancers felt themselves disciplined instruments of precision; their counterparts considered themselves freely creative and self-expressive individuals. They moved differently, felt differently.

The way the human being moves exemplifies certain manners of dealing with time, space, and energy—which amounts to exhibiting manners of dealing with the world, because those elements constitute the system of constraints with which we all have to cope. In this sense we necessarily relate to the dancer as a person. He displays a way of dealing with the world that we find congenial or admirable or distasteful. But if the manner is neutral, bland, if the style is dull, we feel no involvement. For the dancer to execute the visible dimensions of the prescribed steps is not enough; that is only part of the style. The style lies also in the attitude toward the movement, which is also an attitude toward life.

Rayner Heppenstall stated that the classical style of ballet reflects what is "thought most significant in the culture of the West." He specified the qualities he considered distinctive: extroverted, expansive, centrifugal, objective. With these properties, he asserted, ballet needs no representational interest; it need not compete with drama. In itself, the style is "one epitome of the total history of the West," with its respect for tradition, for order, for "clarity of spirit." Ballet, he noted, "expresses only itself, which is to say, certain general qualities of style."

Still he found these qualities metaphorically representational, an attitude that led David Levin to assert that Heppenstall was pleading for a limited formalism, that of semantics, rather than for a "sweeping formalism in syntax." For Heppenstall the tensions of ballet subsist in the struggle between tradition and the free human being, between the demands of impersonality and precision and the individual free will; these reflect the tensions of life. For Levin, on the contrary, the opposing drives are self-referring. Stressing the tension between weight and weightlessness as "the essence of the ballet art," Levin found that when this essence is "properly isolated, exhibited, and—in a word—released, it can be exquisitely expressive entirely on its own." Without mimesis, without "symbolic convention," the style is significant. Such arguments were not advanced with regard to the early modern dance, though they have become prevalent with regard to its later manifestations.

Does this mean that eventually, as the talk was going a few

years ago, the two genres might merge? Certainly we have seen signs of growing similarity as both ballet and modern dance concentrate on themes of pure movement. We find such titles as Choo San Goh's *Momentum*, Glen Tetley's *Circles*, Douglas Dunn's *Gestures in Red*, and Molissa Fenley's *Energizer*, the first two called ballet, the last two modern dance. But representation or lack of it is a critical determinant, not of a genre of dance, but of a species within such a genre. The central factor must relate to the movement. Can the movement qualities be merged?

In the 1970s Clive Barnes called attention to the trend in modern dance of incorporating elements of technical display, which had always distinguished the ballet. Now, while no style can be simultaneously predominantly light and weighted, goal-oriented and path-focused, there is nothing in the nature of modern dance that invariably prohibits the exhibition of technical skill. However, skill does weaken a dramatic work when it detracts attention from emotional expressiveness (which is also true of ballet) or when it is used with qualities that are antithetical to the genre. The trouble with some recent performances of early modern dance works stems especially from the latter of these: the lithe bodies of today's dancers fail to attack their movements with sufficient force, with sufficient weight, for that particular style. The result is not a merging but an incongruity. Aware of the danger, Graham changed the costumes for her revival of *Primitive Mysteries*, adding a ruffle to the formerly plain skirt, a softening that would have clashed with the austere, angular performance of 1931, but that was entirely appropriate to the milder approach of the dancers of 1964. Lightness and the early modern dance simply cannot be merged.

Lightness, however, suits Cunningham, though he uses it in an unballetic way. Arlene Croce has suggested that, for aerial movement, he substitutes "incredibly rapid shifts of weight and direction, and packed staccato changes of pace on the ground." He modifies other classical qualities as well. The dancer establishes a still, vertical center but quickly moves off it into perilous off-balance positions, into asymmetrical configurations. Sometimes the Cunningham phrase takes on some of the smoothness of balletic flow; at other times, like a good image in metaphysical poetry, heterogeneous movements seem linked together by violence; at still other times the flow appears simply discursive. Cunningham dancers tend to be balletically precise, skilled, impersonal. When a critic admitted that he was confused by David Vaughan's apparently equal enthusiasm for Cunningham and Ashton, Vaughan remarked that he found their work equally marked by purity, austerity, clarity, and rigor. Perhaps we would be better off in describing dance works if we looked for such qualities instead of grabbing for the nearest available label.

Labels are useful when they lead the viewer to what is actually present in the dance, but misleading when they call attention exclusively to traits that it shares with others of somewhat the same ilk, often to the detriment of the very properties that distinguish it as an especially important creation. The situation is particularly risky at this moment when the dance scene comprises so many diverse approaches. But we are not entirely safe when we rely on labels to describe the past either. Take the case of *Swan Lake.*

Swan Lake exhibits the classical style at its height: its movement is predominantly marked by outwardness, verticality, skill, clarity, objectivity, grace. True, we have already noted the drooping gestures of Odette and the forcefulness of Odile, but these are the more striking for being exceptional in this conventional movement setting. The divergencies draw attention to the ballerina, who otherwise sustains the balletic qualities. The atypicality contributes to characterization but does not violate the style.

The national dances in the second act also serve as a foil. They are notably unauthentic, for the originally earthy steps are here tamed and refined, so that the contrast is not too extreme and they do not appear out of place at the Queen's ball. This involves a selection of classical qualities, for lightness and delicacy would appear incongruous with the weighted and energetic movements that belong to the czardas and mazurka that are called for here. Clarity and skill, however, are not inconsistent; they "balleticize" the folk dance steps without infringing on their character. On the other hand, Yuri Grigorovich's decision to have the national dances performed on pointe by the Bolshoi Ballet disturbed many observers, and with reason, for his choice, in addition to making the stylistic divergence less notable and therefore less interesting, employed the very qualities most inconsistent with the peasant aura—lightness and delicacy.

Certain verbs of motion, then, seem naturally to enjoy the company of certain others, but not all such relationships are inevitably congenial. In *Swan Lake*, the cordial affiliations used by Petipa were well established and accepted by the St. Petersburg of his day; those of Ivanov were more inventive, though not drastically so. The addition of a new quality or two to a standard vocabulary hardly constitutes a major stylistic revolution. But revolutions, like the one instigated by the modern dance in this century, are as infrequent as they are thrilling, and as conspicuous. Less obvious are the changes that occur—sometimes almost imperceptibly—as a style gradually absorbs new qualities into its traditional format. Still short of revolution are the infusions that tend to irritate by their unfamiliarity in a familiar context; they intrude on the well-known formula, challenging the viewer to adust his perceptive apparatus when he is least expecting to have to do so. (The reception of Balanchine's early choreography in America is a case in point.) With the heralded revolutionary, the observer is better prepared, though this does not necessarily make acceptance any easier. At their greatest, both ballet and modern dance are comprised of a number of subtle and complex styles, which urge us to relinquish our neat, comfortable havens of fixed categories for the hazardous but rewarding shores of the aesthetically unknown.

Balletic joy. Anne Sonnerup, Arne Bech, Vivi Flindt, and Mette Hønningen leap exuberantly in August Bournonville's *Napoli*. *Photo by Mira.*

Modern joy. Ruth Andrien, Robert Kahn, and Carolyn Adams are more contained, delighting in their contact with the earth, in Paul Taylor's *Aureole*. *Photo by Susan Cook.*

Grief in José Limón's *The Moor's Pavane*. Can ballet dancer Erik Bruhn (right) match the intensity of Limón himself? *Limón photo by Daniel Lewis. Bruhn photo by Martha Swope.*

7. LEBEDINOE OZERO
by Any Other Name

American Ballet Theatre production of *Swan Lake. Photo by Mira.*

WHETHER it is called *Lebedinoe Ozero* or *Lac des Cygnes* or *Svanesøen* or *Lago dei Cigni* or *Schwanensee* or *Swan Lake*, it is with us and seems likely to stay around for some time to come. It is here but it is never the same; no two performances are ever exactly alike and some practically challenge our powers of recognition. Yet we seem to have this idea of a work by which we measure any particular performance as a good or bad realization or—possibly—not as a true realization at all but rather a betrayal of the real *Swan Lake*.

We have seen that ideas about dance, about what constitutes its values and its attractions, what should be praised and what denounced, have evolved over the centuries. Since the 1895 premiere of the Ivanov-Petipa *Swan Lake* our ideas have been altered by events that have affected every aspect of our world, and naturally they have changed the course of dance. Even within the sphere of ballet we have seen a tremendous acceleration of technical advances. Not only have the classical steps been stretched and multiplied, but the vocabulary has been enriched (or vulgarized, depending on one's point of view) with additions from such freer movement fields as "modern dance" and jazz. We have seen a shift—though not a universally accepted one—from an emphasis on ballet as a vehicle for a star performer to ballet as the creative work of a great choreographer. We have witnessed expansions in the scope of acceptable subjects, from the princely hero of *Sleeping Beauty* to those guys-next-door sailors of Robbins's *Fancy Free*; from the playful romance of *La Fille Mal Gardée* to the psychodrama of Tudor's *Undertow*; from the involved plots of the nineteenth century to the plotless works of Balanchine.

The audience has changed as well, and it tends to have trouble with dance works that do not mirror the values of a society like its own. Arlene Croce has discussed works that no longer excite us because "their aesthetic is dead . . . the life of the period that produced them has receded and they're insulated from the way we think and move today." Yet their status may not be fixed, for another decade, equipped with still another set of values, may find the same work pleasantly accessible. This does not, however, mean that they will view it with the eyes of the original audience. The attitude is bound to differ; nostalgia is frequently involved, as is benign amusement. The work may succeed with this audience, but not for the same reasons that it succeeded in its own time.

Jerrold Levinson urges that we at least attempt to recapture the experience of the original audience, suggesting that the appropriate frame of mind for hearing period music might be engendered with the aid of some relevant information and a bit of imagination. In theory this could certainly be applied to dance, though it would take some doing. Dance audiences tend to ignore program notes, though as a matter of fact they would learn very little from what is generally provided for them. A valiant effort was made in England by Peter Brinson's Ballet for All company, which presented historical repertory in a lecture-demonstration format, but no such wide-ranging project has been attempted in America. The recently burgeoning interest in reviving dances from the past has seldom been accompanied by the provision of adequate information for the audience, though some magazine articles along with radio and television interviews have allowed directors like Robert Joffrey to describe the background of historical works in their current repertories.

But using information supplied for the occasion, while it will certainly help us to understand what happens on the stage and to some extent to appreciate it, cannot guarantee a duplication of the original experience. Yes, we may recapture some of it—and this is a marvelous step forward—but we are forever denied the experience of the original effect, if only because the first audience perceived the work naturally, with knowledge and feelings shared by all their contemporaries, who lived in the same society and were attuned to the same manner of perceiving. Perhaps the modern spectator is somewhat like the visitor from a foreign country; he has learned the language but only in rare cases can he respond to it in a manner similar to that of the native. We may, however, enjoy an experience denied to the original viewers, for with the acquisition of historical background comes a certain sense of awe, a thrill engendered by the thinking, as we gaze at *The Whims of Cupid and the Ballet Master* (1786), that we are seeing choreography that has been handed down for nearly two hundred years. If we know something about the state of eighteenth-century dance, we accept the ballet's apparent lack of technical challenge. We accept its conventions as a sign of its historicity and enjoy them as such. But we must realize that this is not the experience enjoyed by the audience of 1786. Will we ever thrill again to the modest arabesque, to the fleet but delicate brisés of a bygone era? Our response is not likely to be excited, but it can be pleasurable nonetheless.

What concerns us most, however, is to find those qualities that make a great work of art timeless in its appeal. Rosen has suggested for the study of musical practice that the point "is not to unearth the authentic traditions of performance and to lay down rules, but to strip away the accretions of the traditions of the past (including those accepted by the composer himself) and the fashion and taste of the present—all of which get in the way of music more often than not." They may get in the way of dance, too. Sometimes an overly scrupulous application of historical research may lead us astray. Historical and aesthetic values do not always coincide and they are frequently confused. Some older dances, if they could be reconstructed, would be more suitable for display in a museum than on the stage. A work may be wonderfully revealing of the temper and taste of a nation or era, providing insights into the nature of a society that could help to explain any number of other events of the time, but as art it may be minor or even deplorable.

This makes a good argument for preserving everything we can in notation or on film. Theatrical production is something else again.

For the museum, accuracy is a primary requisite. We want to see the original staging or the closest possible replica of it. After all, we have come in order to learn about the past. But the theatrical situation, while it may provide delight for its audience with the rarity of a historical revival, must nevertheless face additional pressures to give the spectator an experience commensurate with his expectations, which are not apt to be purely educational. This may be at least partially resolved by a carefully prepared manner of presentation, or it may require some compromise. Yet we should proceed cautiously. It is possible that in some cases historical and theatrical values just might coincide.

Randall Dipert distinguishes three levels of intention concerning the production of musical sound: the first designates the type of instrument and fingering; the second specifies such aspects as timbre, attack, and vibrato; the third defines the effect to be produced in the listener. Fidelity to one of the first two, Dipert asserts, may violate the third, as when a sound that was startling to a former era is reproduced exactly, although the pattern is now dull from familiarity and cannot impress today's listener very much. Levinson, however, claims that this argument confuses the work with the spirit of the work, granting that a performance which is faithful to the spirit while violating the text may be more rewarding to a modern audience than a correct performance. Are we concerned with the precise steps originally assigned to the dancer or with the effect that they originally had on their audience? What was most important to the choreographer?

Regardless of what the choreographers wished to produce artistically they had to meet certain demands placed on them by the St. Petersburg of 1895. Technically and ideologically, a ballet had to please the tsar and his entourage, various levels of the nobility, visiting dignitaries, and fervent local balletomanes. The story had to justify the designing of some lavish costumes and spectacular scenic effects. The large corps de ballet had to be used, and promising young soloists had to be given opportunities. Most important, however, was the display of the ballerina. The ballet was a vehicle to exhibit her particular skills. Such demands may seem to involve only ulterior motives for the composers, but they were not inconsequential; on the contrary, they determined some of the most significant features of the choreography.

Let us say that the work is composed and rehearsed and performed and it is a success. The following season the director of the theatre asks that it again be included in the repertory. But the guest ballerina, who had the starring role, is no longer available. The usual demands are still present, but the talents of a different dancer have to be displayed. Possibly last year's variations will suit her, but more likely they will not show her to greatest advantage. What to do? One possibility is to choreograph new dances for her, and probably some will be done. Another choice is to let the lady perform something she already knows and has rendered with success. It comes from another ballet? No matter. The style of the period is sufficiently homogeneous that even the work of another choreographer is not likely to seem intrusive. The audience will be happy to see a favorite variation again. Besides, who remembers where it first appeared? Local color was immaterial, because this was provided by the decor and the costumes of the corps, who would be given a character dance or two to establish the milieu; the ballerina would wear her usual tutu and dance the steps of the classical vocabulary in the classical style while the story waited.

In its time, this was the attitude taken toward *Swan Lake*; individual dances were rechoreographed as demanded by cast changes, sequences were changed, characters came and went. No one then cried that the Sacred Work had been violated. To comply strictly with the intentions of the choreographers on this level could involve rechoreographing the role of Odette/Odile for each new ballerina who assumed the role. Actually, this has been done far more often for Odile than for Odette, which may lead us to wonder if, at least in practice, attitudes might vary depending on the style of the choreography.

Odile is especially vulnerable because she is the epitome of the performer-oriented role. As Verdi composed an individual cabaletta for each singer who attempted a single aria, so Petipa might well have devised a virtuoso enchaînement other than the fouettés for a ballerina other than Legnani (if he did not do so for Mathilde Kchessinskaya, when she took over the role, this was because she wanted the audience to know that she had mastered that very trick). The part of Odette, however, used Legnani in a manner contrary to type—lyrically, poetically. It was as if Ivanov's response to the music overcame his duty-bound call to show her in brilliant pyrotechnics. The integration of movement, music, and expression in the acts of *Swan Lake* that he choreographed superseded the stylistic norm for the place and period. It is that integration, especially in the famous adagio, that makes the substitution of material elements so difficult. The folding and unfolding of the body of the swan queen matches the ebb and flow of the music; it also reveals her ambivalent attitude toward Siegfried—she both wants his love and fears it. Odette softly drops her head toward one shoulder and the other, then holds it high over her arched back; the prince opens her arms, then closes them beneath his own; she reaches out with one leg, then brings it gently in as she turns on pointe. A viewing of films of some dozen different performances of this adagio showed only minor variations; some ballerinas had higher extensions, some turned more multiple pirouettes. Only when the deviations verged on flamboyant virtuosity was the spell broken. Similar films of the Odile portions exhibited drastic differences, yet none of them appeared seriously inappropriate. Bournonville remarked of bravura numbers that "they belong to their own times and to the personalities by whom they are performed and eventually become obsolete, whereas those which denote character retain their freshness and significance." I really cannot argue with that.

Jack Anderson suggests that the difference may be in the eye of the beholder. Some viewers are idealists, considering effect as the criterion for the identity of the work; materialists, however, insist that the identity lies in the particular steps or sequences of movements, whether or not they produce the identical effect from performance to performance. In his terms, I am sometimes an idealist, sometimes a materialist.

I am a materialist when I consider Tudor's *Pillar of Fire*. The curtain rises to reveal Hagar sitting stiffly erect on the porch of her Victorian house. One hand begins to tug at her high, tight collar. Clearly she is suffocating from the rigid mores of her environment. The image could not be more apt, and I cannot imagine time changing its impact. Another case: Humphrey's *Day on Earth*. The child has grown up and gone away; the mother folds the white sheet on which her daughter was born. With each fold her body contracts in a silent sob; a simple domestic action has become a symbol of the end of a phase of the inevitable life cycle. That is the way Letitia Ide performed it. Unfortunately, the contraction is no longer visible, and the gesture has lost its impact.

Sometimes any movement would be a sacrilege. In Bournonville's *The King's Volunteers on Amager*, there is the poignant stillness of the ballroom as Louise removes her mask and her husband realizes he has been flirting with his own wife. Or the famous "freeze" in Tudor's *Lilac Garden*, when Caroline stands between the man she loves and the man she must marry, finally realizing that she must make an irrevocable choice.

While such dramatic passages are probably the most vulnerable, they are not alone in making demands. Some movement styles depend for their identity on the observance of very specific kinds of spatial, temporal, and dynamic patterns. There is the case of the original step stripped of its ornamentation—surely a minor matter. But take the Bournonville batterie—those small, swift interlacings that give the movement its filigree quality. There is no problem in changing an entrechat six to an entrechat huit (providing the dancer can do it with ease and lightness), but reduce the entrechat to a plain changement and the style is betrayed. Another special mark of Bournonville: the charming pirouette en dedans, which concludes many of his pas de deux and variations. Originally a double turn on demi-pointe, it is not harmed by becoming a triple on pointe. But a pirouette en dehors will not do. The Danish dancers modestly fold in on themselves before gently offering their respects to the audience. The Russians proudly turn outward, throwing their bravura to the gallery.

Some kinds of dances, however, induce me into being more of an idealist. Works of virtuosity contribute the largest number of examples to this category, but other, largely nondramatic works also figure prominently because their style is looser, the range broader. What matters then may be a mood, a pattern of musical response, a characteristic visual design. Jerome Robbins remarked of a revival of his *Interplay* that it was practically the same, but he had added a few steps to suit the talents of the new dancers. As long as the spirit of fun, of delight in the play of classical steps against syncopated rhythms is maintained, the choice of which classical steps is comparatively open. Yet when Leonide Massine revived his *Parade*, he admitted that he had forgotten many of the steps and changed others deliberately in terms of what seemed appropriate to him at the moment. But Robert Joffrey insisted on the most faithful reproduction of the Picasso costumes, which may well have been the one absolutely constituent element of the ballet.

Now certain kinds of flexibility may actually form the essence of the dance work. In the mid 1960s Cunningham began his series of "events," which took parts of dances already composed and strung them together in a continuous flow of movement that lasted sixty to ninety minutes. Some of his dances, the choreographer remarked, could not be worked into events because they had been built as entities, while others had been initially composed as sets of independent units. Yet the fragmentation occasioned by the event format did not violate the identity of the individual works: "In a sense I try very hard to keep the shape and whatever 'givenness' I thought a piece had. . . . I try to keep whatever quality that particular piece has." Cunningham equated "shape" with "sense," noting that the "content" of his dances is "the phrasing, the structure and the actual physical nature of the movement." Despite what has been said about the arbitrary nature of Cunningham's principles of organization, they seem actually to be more rigorous than those of the popular ballet of the late nineteenth century.

Not all contemporary choreographers are as rigorous as Cunningham, or they are not rigorous in the same way. Trisha Brown, for example, uses tasks, pieces of equipment, or problem-solving devices to structure her dances. In *Sticks*, five women manipulate a line of long sticks that must be kept in end-to-end contact while they perform a series of simple movements that vary unpredictably as they are interrupted by attempts to keep the sticks in line. The style of the dance lies not in the quality but rather in the function of the movement. In such dances, when we ask if they have been correctly performed, the observance of rules becomes the determining factor. Depending on the instructions, such factors as the number of dancers, the nature of their movements, their use of the performing area, as well as matters of rhythm and tempo and the total length of the piece itself may vary from one performance to the next.

Remy Charlip's mail-order dances can look quite dissimilar in execution by different performers because their identity lies only in a series of drawings of still positions that have been mailed to the dancer, who then devises whatever movement he wishes to link the positions to one another (though the directions vary somewhat in their degree of specification).

In some contemporary works the performer is a collaborator

with the choreographer. For *Lazy Madge*, Douglas Dunn made a set of solos and duets that his dancers performed. Subsequently he made some additional duets and group pieces that could be, but did not have to be, added to the set, since for each performance the dancers decided which units to dance or not to dance, and if to dance them, then where and when. The movement sequences were chosen from an established (but also expanding) range of possibilities; the structures varied with each performance. Dunn was solely responsible for the material, the dancers for its organization. Other choreographers ask their dancers to share in the creation of the movements, which are discovered through sessions of group improvisation, then subsequently structured by the choreographer. Or they proceed like Kenneth King: "I'm constantly trying to let the dancers make decisions. In order to do that, the dancers have to be aware of the design or concept to be able to know what the options are at certain points." Some contemporary dances, then, may be defined in terms of their adherence to ground rules which, in turn, may apply to the shape of the steps, the ordering of the sequences, the quality of the movement, or any other factor so designated by the choreographer. But he does designate; there are always rules.

Thinkers about dance tend to envy their musical counterparts who can work from written scores. Nevertheless—even apart from the puzzles posed by early notation systems—the function of the musical score has stimulated vociferous debates on the part of theorists. One side holds that the score is sacred; the performer is only a necessary medium between the work and the audience, his aim to put the observer in contact with the work, allowing as little intrusion of his own alien personality as possible. Ideally, the listener should feel himself relating to the composer and not the performer. The other side holds that the score itself leaves much to the discretion of the performer, that the notation is not adequate to provide precise instructions and furthermore such precision would be undesirable, since it would limit the player to such an extent that every performance of the music would sound almost exactly alike. Such a score would prevent the exploration of the myriad possibilities for interpreting the work—in Dufrenne's terms, the exploration of its multiple truths.

Scores can be used in dance, not as the final arbiter of detail, but as the designator of those constituent properties that are necessary to any realization of the particular work. Margolis contends that it is not requisite for different performances of a dance to exhibit a common set of necessary and sufficient features, illustrating his claim with reference to the nineteenth-century practice of basing choreography on the personal styles of the dancers. Consistently with this approach, the style would change as new dancers took on the roles. Some dances, he asserts, may be more stylistically tolerant than others, citing a balletic rendition of *The Moor's Pavane*, which happened to have failed but for which he found "no antecedent reason to preclude a classical rendition." But his example is an especially unfortunate one, since the use of balletic qualities cancels the very traits that identify Limón's choreography—power of passion, tension of fear, weight of remorse. Further, while nineteenth-century practice was indeed star-oriented, this accounts only for its initiating motivation. The style thus produced has a quality of its own that can be perceived and enjoyed quite apart from any knowledge of the circumstances of its origin. Stylistically tolerant is one thing a dance cannot be— unless it has no distinctive character. A notated score can indicate exactly those features that constitute style, the features that any performance must exhibit in order to be an instance of the work.

Armelagos and Sirridge claim that a notated score can record only "steps," while style involves "spatial vocabulary," which is "an inventory of acceptable positions and position sequences," and "kinesthetic motivation," which relates to "the pattern of the movement flow, the originating impulse." According to the authors, these elements constitute style, and style is "the ultimate criterion" of the work. However, Labanotation, combined with

Effort/Shape analysis, is quite capable of indicating both the vocabulary and the motivation. It can also record a number of critical
factors not mentioned by Armelagos and Sirridge. Surely, the use
of time is as significant to style as the use of space, though they
designate only the latter. Further, the authors seem concerned
only with the activity of a single person moving in a kind of
vacuum, but this would make some usually key questions
strangely irrelevant. Is the performing area sparse or crowded, do
the dancers touch one another or does each move in isolation, are
the patterns symmetrical, how do solo passages relate to ensembles? The answers may point to stylistic features that are essential
to the identity of the work.

Of course, dance notation does not directly describe a work's
stylistic structure; like the musical score, it contains particular
signs that, taken together, indicate the structure. With a very few
exceptions, most choreographers do not want the scores of their
works to be rigidly binding on the dancers; they expect adjustments to be made in accordance with the technical abilities of the
performers and they do not prohibit the possibility of a personality
shining through. The score should, however, specify the range
allowed to the dancer's interpretation. Marcia Siegel claims that
"whenever an early dance is reclaimed from someone's memory,
both dancers and audience want to see it modernized, at least to
the extent of fitting it out with today's long-legged, presentational
performing style." But what if that style is inconsistent with the
style indicated by the score?

There are limits, and the study of a well-made score will reveal
them. Unless the work is utterly eclectic, the notated steps will
show a family resemblance that neither regisseur nor dancer should
venture to violate. The score can provide evidence of the structure
and quality of the movement that most often define a dance. It
can also be adjusted to serve the variety of conceptual schemes
being used today, though in some cases a paragraph of standard
prose or a mathematical formula might serve as well or perhaps

better. However, a score does not, and I think should not, specify every detail of performance—unless it is intended for a museum and not for production. Most of us go to see a repertory work in the theatre (as opposed to a film) in order to experience a fresh interpretation, to encounter a new truth of the work that will reveal another facet of its richness. There may be a number of ways to interpret correct, score-correlated movement; on the other hand, some ways are definitely incorrect. Structure and quality as signified by the score delimit the range of acceptable performing style.

Factors other than written directions may also be significant, especially in the case of historical works. Anthropologists urge us to treat dances like artifacts. To understand them we must understand their original context, the society in which and for which they were made, trying to recover the ideas, the motivations that gave birth to the work. At the time of its creation there was no need to indicate such matters as when and how to smile at one's partner—accepted mores dictated the decision. Period stylization was the norm and required no particular specification. Now these matters must be discovered in peripheral sources—contemporary books of etiquette, pictures, diaries.

Some performers, however, have their reservations about this approach, doubting that—despite the best of intentions—they could adequately absorb the mental, emotional, and physical habits of another era. Dinna Bjørn commented on the problems of dancing Bournonville's mid-nineteenth-century choreography in the last quarter of the twentieth century: "If I were to try dancing Bournonville as I imagine he was danced during his lifetime . . . I would have to dance in a way that felt somewhat unnatural to me."

Knowing that to Bournonville dance meant joy, ease, and naturalness, she considered her goal as performing his steps "in a completely natural and spontaneous way." Here she felt that complete material fidelity would lead to betrayal of the spirit. Which does not imply that the dancer should ignore the material. Erik Bruhn considered the matter carefully, concluding that, "when I think of Bournonville I have to go on from where I see him, and that's from inside me. It is not what others have done. I have to do it from myself. Of course we can learn from others and their experiences with him. But if we are to recreate his spirit through the technique he left us all, we must understand him in our present time." Such performers may be accused of taking undue liberties. But they will remind the objector of how many elements in the production as a whole have already been altered: the theatre has been modernized, the scenery and costumes were recently renovated, the mime scenes were abbreviated long ago when audiences had become bored with them. Furthermore, the eyes that watch them tonight are familiar, not with the technique of Legnani and Gerdt but with that of Farrell and Baryshnikov. Opinions differ about what is necessary, preferable, conceivable to reach today's audience without violating the work.

Historical values dictate that insofar as possible the choreography should be saved. Certainly this should be done for our museum exhibition. But what about the theatre? Rosen warns that sometimes old music should be played "wrong." We should not try to save an idea just because it was original; it might have been a bad idea that worked at the time only because of the bad taste of the audience. We know that certain decisions were made with regard to *Swan Lake* for purposes that were largely pragmatic: Benno was added to the adagio to help the aging Gerdt, who lacked the strength to support the ballerina; thirty-two fouettés were included for Legnani because the audience would have been furious if they had been denied the sight of this famous display. The two cases are not identical.

What is Benno if not a tradition inherited from an accident of practical necessity? I have heard his function defended—he shows Odette to Siegfried, displays her to him before relinquishing her. But prior to that moment, Siegfried has let her fall right into

Benno's arms. Why? I confess I am unconvinced. Given that he had to use Benno, Ivanov used him with grace. He does not detract from the proceedings stylistically, which makes him an acceptable addition to *Swan Lake* if not an essential one.

The fouettés are another matter because, as we have seen, they serve a positive dramatic function. The only question here is: Could another step serve that function equally well? For our time, perhaps, could another step serve it even better?

Odile could be doing them to dazzle the prince (even though he is not looking) or she could be exulting in her already achieved triumph over him. Either way, what works here is movement that is brilliant, strong, and positive. Lyrical swooping around will not do; softness would be out of place. This woman knows what she wants and she has the skills to get it. These qualities her movement must have or it is inappropriate to her character and situation. Other qualities may be added—this would be a matter of interpretation—but they would have to be consistent with the essential ones. Especially problematical now is the factor of brilliance, which, as we have seen, various ballerinas have solved by updating the fouettés through ornamentation. Ornamentation—Bayer's broderies—enhances the vision of the very qualities deemed essential, and Odile is strong enough, free enough, that she can play with the virtuoso feat. This is not really troublesome. I see no reason to consider these broderies as a fundamental alteration.

But supposing the ballerina—an exquisite swan in every other respect—does not do good fouettés. She struggles valiantly, but still they look rather sad, the whipping leg drooping lower with each revolution, the arms thrown around in desperation, the supporting foot sometimes making it to the pointe, sometimes not. Where now is Odile, the confident, triumphant seductress? Well, the dancer has quite simply destroyed the illusion. Or if we want to say that the illusion is unimportant, that the audience is really looking at a mere performer rather than a character and knows it, hasn't she still failed? Her function is to show us that she can do what we cannot, defy the threats of gravity and vertigo, proclaim her conquest of time and space, thrill us with a vision of the potential of ambition. But there is nothing exciting about a fumbling Odile; human awkwardness is a common sight. Would it not, then, perhaps, be better to let this performer do something else, something that she does supremely well, something that will thrill the audience as much as the fouettés done by someone else?

Take the case of the piqué tours en manège performed by Maya Plisetskaya. They are still turns and they are still fast, but they circumscribe the stage space instead of remaining on one spot. Even more important, they involve a different kind of body design: in the fouettés the working leg is fully extended, waist high to the side, before it is drawn in sharply to whip the body around. In the piqué tour the leg reaches out just above the floor and just enough to effect an easy transfer of weight in addition to progress along a circular path. The assertive extension and the emphatic inward directed motion are eliminated and with them the self-centered image that proclaims the true character of Odile. Still, the piqués can be performed with power and clear determination. They are on the right track.

Must the dancer do a form of pirouette? Wouldn't any brilliant feat do the trick? How about back flips? They are certainly virtuosic; they could be performed to the same music. The fact that most ballet dancers cannot do them is irrelevant. Or is it?

Ballet training was designed to produce an instrument fit for classical style—open, light, brilliant. These qualities pervade ballet choreography unless, for good reasons, they are deliberately violated, as in character roles and comedy bits. If *Swan Lake* is to be dominated by these qualities, transgressions need justification. How can we justify those back flips? The motion looks curiously self-contained, because the eyes can focus on neither audience nor prince; the body simply moves as a unit unto itself. There is also something coarse about the upside-down position, with head directed to the floor, legs in the air. Balanchine used it to exactly this purpose when he had the Siren in *The Prodigal Son* walk in the bridge position, kicking up each leg alternately as her hands support her weight. This, however, does not suit Odile, who has been a most elegant seductress. She is far too dignified to sacrifice her regal erectness to a cheap trick. The Siren's effort works for the Prodigal, who is not a prince but a naive and bewildered boy, utterly duped by this vulgar display. But Siegfried is noble and mature enough to be truly in love and even to sacrifice himself in the end for that love. If he were so fickle, so easily entrapped by a woman so unlike the refined Odette, he would lose our respect and our sympathy. Steps embody style which manifests character; back flips would betray the style of *Swan Lake* and the character of Odile.

Classical style places limits on the range of steps suitable for its dancers, but the scope remaining is wide. Even within its strict vocabulary—not considering the boundaries to which it has been stretched in the past few decades—there is extensive latitude for both choreographer and performer. An arabesque is an arabesque, and a higher or faster arabesque is only a matter of degree. But at a certain point—though still an arabesque—it has changed from demure to audacious. Odette's arabesque is pliant and melting; Odile's is sharp and bold. Even fouettés, Odile's aggressively triumphant signature, are transformed for Odette, who modestly does just a few of them, quite slowly, while supported by her prince.

For dance, movement quality and structure are bound to be constituent factors, though the aspect of quality or structure that is crucial in any particular instance may vary considerably. More energy here, less tension there, may or may not make a difference. Consider the use of spacious gesture by the repressed characters of Anna Sokolow's *Rooms*, weighted attack in lighthearted *Coppélia*, goal-oriented directness in Tharp's quirky *Deuce Coupe*. Betrayals all. What would happen to Balanchine's *Tombeau de*

Couperin if it were performed with the dancers constantly facing front instead of constantly interweaving in the patterns of the contredanse? What would happen to a work by Laura Dean if the full range of movements were executed one by one successively instead of each being repeated—twenty, fifty, a hundred times? What if the easy pace of Robbins's *Dances at a Gathering*—with its deliciously casual encounters, its luxuriant development of movement nuances—were hurried into a tight, nervous presto?

While we may contend that movement quality and structure are the most essential elements in a dance work, they are not always the exclusive determining factors. Some dances are representational, and this is neither accidental nor peripheral. It is, in fact, a matter of style and as such may be a constituent property. When Eliot Feld took the characteristic cowboy gestures, familiar to audiences from Eugene Loring's *Billy the Kid* and Agnes de Mille's *Rodeo*, but eliminated narrative sequence in favor of kinetic structure, he produced *Excursions*, an entirely different kind of work, one that focused on the intrinsic quality of the movements rather than on the depiction of character or emotion. A dance that takes as its subject the manifestation of its own movement qualities is fundamentally distinct from one that uses its medium for purposes of representation or expression.

The revival of a dramatic work poses its own particular problems, as it must take into account a special kind of change in taste. The accommodating variation of a few details may be inconsequential: some of the mime is omitted; Siegfried's character is more or less serious from the beginning; even a happy ending is not entirely inconsistent, as the original finale included an apotheosis with the couple united in an idyllic afterlife. But turning Rothbart into an alter-ego of Siegfried's mother or the prince into the mad Ludwig of Bavaria gives an entirely different tone to the proceedings. As does the scene of Rudolf Nureyev on the shores of "Swine Lake" where, shocked to discover that his beloved has turned into a fluffy-tutued pig, he tries to get rid of her and, much to his relief, finally sees her whisked off to Muppet heaven. Then there is Prince Sigmund, enchanted by Yvette—she is half swan and half woman, divided lengthwise—who tells him that "she is under a spell cast by a magician named Von Epps, and that because of her appearance it is nearly impossible to get a bank loan. In an especially difficult solo, she explains, in dance language, that the only way to lift Von Epps' curse is for her lover to go to secretarial school." Woody Allen had the courtesy to title his scenario "A Spell."

Less obvious but often no less significant are shifts in emphasis that indicate a changed attitude toward the events of the plot, which may be taken more or less seriously, romantically, realistically. Vera Krasovskaya has commented on Vladimir Bourmeister's staging of *Swan Lake*, with its prologue explaining the transformation of Odette and its use of everyday gesture in the scene of Siegfried's birthday party. For Krasovskaya, such attention to literal detail destroys the poetic universality of Ivanov's symphonic structure. Yet this trend to specificity has characterized a number of recent productions: Siegfried has become more "human," his personality more defined; the character dances in the ball scene have been contrived with dramatic "motivation." The outline of the story remains intact, but a predominantly lyrical work is made into a rather prosaically narrative one.

Almost any theatrical element may be used in a manner that makes it essential to dance, but no general rule can hold for all cases. A dance work deserves to be considered on its own terms, and the contemporary scene offers a wide variety of examples. For instance, there is Paul Taylor's *Polaris*, which tested the status of music by having the same steps performed to different scores (the cast and the lighting were also changed). In response to the music, the movement in the second version became stronger, more percussive, as if what had been gentle searchings were transformed into aggressive attacks. The effect was drastically different, though I could conceive of these two halves as two aspects of the same dance.

Costume may most often be considered a contingent property, but some years ago when Balanchine put the dancers of *Chopiniana* into short tunics instead of the usual long skirts, there were cries of "sacrilege!" Nancy Goldner, however, found the change brought out "the choreography's precision and deliberateness. . . .The placement of the dancers now looks more linear, lending to the pretty formations a welcome touch of austerity." Austerity was not a romantic virtue, but in the 1970s prettiness was out of fashion. Still, one could argue that prettiness was a constitutent property of the ballet and that the linear look, while it could produce a statement more acceptable to the contemporary audience, could also negate the tenor of the original.

We would probably be wise not to limit the kind of ingredients that may be essential to a dance. On occasion, words may be necessary. In David Gordon's *What Happened*, a dancer raises four fingers to accompany a spoken "for," the hand passes down over the face to the sound of "avail," a hunched swoop goes with "which." Without the words, the motions would lack, not only their witty meaning, but significant design of any kind. The works of Alwin Nikolais provide now-classic examples of dances that require specific mechanical devices. Here the inanimate shapes and colors move as much or more than the human performers; they are true choreographic elements. Slide projections are essential to Nelson Goodman's *Hockey Seen*, in which Martha Armstrong Gray's dancers are seen against a changing background of Katharine Sturgis's drawings of the game which set the various stages of the action.

Yet in all dances contingencies remain and they provide a gratifying source of flexibility for the performer and a store of new truths for the audience. Change is part of the essence of the performing arts of the west, a factor that places them in juxtaposition to their counterparts in Asia, where individuality counts for little and adherence to established conventions is not only expected but demanded. Within the traditional arts of the east, the problem of *Swan Lake* is simply inconceivable, because variant interpretations are not honored, or are honored only within a very narrow range of compliance. Here we urge the performer to develop his personal concept of a role, enjoying the insight to be gained from a fresh perspective brought to bear on a familiar situation. Thomas Mark contends, I think quite rightly, that in the composition and the performance we have two works of art, both deserving appreciation. Through the imagination of the performer we are led to a new depth of understanding, of vision, which is what we find so rewarding in live theatre.

Sometimes, however, even a western audience resists a new interpretation, conservatively wanting to hold on to a familiar idea rather than venture to grasp a new one. Dufrenne imposes a negative requirement: no one performance should be allowed to establish an exclusive archetype, one that inhibits our acceptance of any other rendering. For some of us there is the persistent memory of Margot Fonteyn's Aurora or Erik Bruhn's Albrecht, which thwarts our capacity to enjoy a number of fine performances because they diverge from the model set by a long-cherished image. Equally threatening—perhaps more so—is the picture implanted by what has come down to us as historical fact. Too often the present fails to measure up to what we have heard or read about the past. Every time the spirit of the rose leaps out of the window he evokes a vision of how Nijinsky might have done it, and that spectre seems to grow more fabulous with each passing year.

Those elements that define a work's abiding identity can be preserved by a notated score, but the work has only a phantom existence until it is realized, brought to life, in performance. Some two centuries ago, James Harris distinguished the performing arts from painting, whose parts coexist in time. In music and dance, "some *Parts* are *ever passing away* and others are ever *succeeding them.*" The painter makes a work that is perceived instantaneously after the energy that created it has ceased. Music and dance, on the contrary, have their "*Being or Essence in a Transition,* call it, what it really is, a *Motion* or an *Energy.*" A dance can be perceived only while its energy is in process; the life of the art work is synchronous with the activity of the performer that makes it available to an audience. Thus the work is continually begotten, born, and dies, only to be reconceived and born again. Though the same steps are executed, they are never the same, because precisely the same combination of circumstances can never recur. In performance and only in performance, the enduring and the ephemeral may become one. Then, indeed, we cannot know the dancer from the dance.

In the case of improvisation, they are actually identical, because the work and its performance come into being simultaneously. The dancer's current mood dictates both. But the relation becomes problematic whenever the situation involves reproducing arrangements that were set previously, even if they were set by the performer himself. Then the identifying properties of the work need to be maintained regardless of what the dancer is feeling at the moment. And here the range of attitudes may vary considerably. At one extreme, the performer considers himself the abject servant, letting his own personality be effaced by the work; at the other extreme, he views the choreography with so little respect that he nearly obliterates the work. The dull dancer is conspicuous by his absence; the superstar outshines everything, including his own role. Both servility and arrogance involve constraint, since either performer or work is forced into a subordinate position, and the observer is uncomfortably aware of the intrusion. There is no question of which is the dancer and which the dance, for the two are obviously, disturbingly distinct.

That now-famous question of William Butler Yeats has been frequently quoted by dance writers who as frequently ignore the fact that it is only the last line of the sixty-four line poem titled "Among School Children." They also seem unaware that the work of Yeats is permeated by recurring, significant images, among them the dancer and the swan.

In the schoolroom a nun explains the curriculum to the poet, who thinks of a beautiful woman, one of the "daughters of the swan." As the lovely image floats (like a swan) into his mind, he recognizes himself as remote from it, "a comfortable kind of old scarecrow." He thinks of the travails of the mother, longing to mold her infant into a beautiful shape, as teachers try to impose a form on their pupils. The process is painful: "Aristotle played the taws/Upon the bottom of a king of kings." It is also futile, for the poet's intellectual endeavors have only turned him into "Old clothes upon old sticks to scare a bird."

Yeats had elsewhere mocked mental exertion. To the dancer who asks if she should go to college, he replies: "Go pluck Athena by the hair;/ For what mere book can grant a knowledge/ With an impassioned gravity/ Appropriate to that beating breast,/ That vigorous thigh, that dreaming eye?" At the sight of the girl who "outdanced thought," he asserts: "Mind moved yet seemed to stop." Understanding comes, not from the intellect but from feeling—the beating heart, the visionary eye. Once these are set in motion, the mind responds, though not in its ordinary manner. Unlike the process of book learning, which separates the functions of body and mind, true knowledge is born of a synthesis. The dancer is like the swan that drifts gracefully on the still waters. Both are "mysterious, beautiful"; they "silence the mind." No more than the beautiful movers themselves can the observer explain the cause of their enchantment. "Labour is blossoming or dancing where/The body is not bruised to pleasure soul." The gift of grace cannot be forced, but it blooms when the recipient responds spontaneously. "O body swayed to music, O brightening glance." The performer becomes one with the persona. "How can we know the dancer from the dance?"

To a real dancer, Yeats' concept is apt to seem unrealistic—their training has afforded them plenty of bruises. All those years at the barre, as Baron's Sophie, the quintessential ballerina, sighed many years ago. Yet in the mature artist the result of his labors so shines as to obliterate any trace of those painful antecedents. What the audience perceives is the exhilaration of identification, as the work is created anew.

That kind of vibrant identification is achieved in performance when the dancer both honors the dance and dares to threaten it with his personal vision. It is the tension that subsists between score and interpretation, between tradition and the claims of individual insight, that generates a special kind of theatrical vitality. When the two blend, the work emerges as the embodiment of a fresh, brightening truth. The danger of the dancer's playing the work false is ever present. Suzanne Farrell has remarked that she wants to be free "to take risks, to be spontaneous . . . rather than repeating the same performance night after night." It is the risks taken, not out of whim, but from deeply felt, nurtured conviction, that bring dances to life. The very nearness of the dividing line—like the state of the virtuoso who hovers on the brink of catastrophe—fires the performance with fresh vitality.

Then—no matter that we have seen her love and lose before—we become involved with the plight of Odette as if we were experiencing it for the first time. No matter that we know the steps of her variation—we gaze in suspense at the floating port de bras, the prolonged arabesque. Siegfried consoles her, and his tenderness extends to all helpless, living things. He leaps at Rothbart and in leaping challenges the aggregate of the powers of evil. It seems that never before have meaning and design, movement and music, come together in quite this way—so individual and impulsive, so exact and inevitable. Here we have discovered a truth of *Swan Lake*. We have also glimpsed its reality.

And this is why we want to see *Swan Lake* again next week—and the week after that and after that.

Left to right: Michael Bloom, Diane Frank, Douglas Dunn; on floor:
Dana Roth in a version of Dunn's *Lazy Madge*. *Photo by Nathaniel Tileston.*

A line from Remy Charlip's "Garden Lilacs." The directions suggest that
each position be held for a long and different time.

Laura Dean Dancers and Musicians in Dean's *Music. Photo by Lois Greenfield.*

Nelson Goodman's *Hocky Seen—A Nightmare in Three Periods and Sudden Death.*
Drawings by Katharine Sturgis; choreography by Martha Armstrong Gray. *Photo
by William J. Rynders.*

Above left: When the movement is not all. Picasso's costumes seen on Donna
Cowen as The Little American Girl with the Manager from New York and the
Horse in the Joffrey Ballet production of Leonide Massine's *Parade. Photo by
Herbert Migdoll.*

Lower left: David Gordon's *What Happened.* Left to right: Margaret Hoeffel,
Susan Eschelbach, Paul Thompson, the choreographer, Valda Setterfield, and
Keith Marshall. *Photo by Nathaniel Tileston.*

Not be be hurried. Bart Cook and Sara Leland in Jerome Robbins' *Dances at a Gathering. Photo by Martha Swope.*

Graham Fletcher tries his wiles on Rudolf Nureyev in "Swine Lake." *Courtesy ITC Entertainment, Inc.*

Gentle maiden/evil sorceress,
Odette/Odille continues to spin
her magic. Natalia Makarova
and Ivan Nagy in the American
Ballet Theatre production, 1971.
Photos by Fred Fehl.

3-16

© 1958, 1963 United Feature Syndicate, Inc.

Notes

Complete data are given for items that are used only for a specific, apposite remark, but are not otherwise relevant to the subject of this book. Articles quoted from anthologies are also detailed here. All other citations are fully documented in the bibliography.

The following abbreviations are used:

BJA   *British Journal of Aesthetics*
BR   *Ballet Review*
DP   *Dance Perspectives*
JAAC   *Journal of Aesthetics and Art Criticism*

Preface

vii. Rosenberg, quoted in "Harold Rosenberg," *The New Yorker,* 24 July 1978, p. 80.

Chapter 1   The Problems of Swan Lake

passim. Information on the early productions of *Swan Lake*, contained in various passages throughout this chapter, is taken from the books and articles by Beaumont, Chujoy, Krasovskaya, Petipa, Slonimsky, and Wiley. For recent productions, I have drawn on my own experience and from clipping files in the Dance Collection of The New York Public Library.

7–8. Ashton and Balanchine in Petipa, pp. 275, 288.

10. Dufrenne. "Can we not," p. 24; "A good rendition," p. 11; "a certain atmosphere," p. 16.

12. Goodman, *Languages,* pp. 116–18.

12. Farrell, quoted in Daniel, pp. 13–14; Ashton in Petipa, p. 275.

13. Laing, quoted in Selma Jeanne Cohen, "Antony Tudor," *DP* 18 (1963): 76; Bell, p. 185.

Chapter 2   Actions and Passions, Airs and Graces

21. Kaeppler, p. 5.

21. Opinions cited in McGrath, p. 82; Ellis, p. 65; Reynolds, p. 124.

22. Opinions cited in Kristeller, passim.

23. Aristotle, *Poetics* 1447a.

23. Beaujoyeulx, "Ballet Comique de la Reine," in Cohen, *Theatre Art,* p. 19. Davies, stanzas 23, 26, 29.

24. Weaver, pp. 160–61.

25. Noverre, "Two Letters on Dancing," in Cohen, *Theatre Art,* p. 62.

25. Gautier, p. 17.

26. Levinson, "The Spirit of the Classic Dance," in Cohen, *Theatre Art,* p. 113; Childs, untitled contribution in Livet, p. 63; Smith, p. 247; anonymous critic, *Spirit of the Times* (New York), 18 September 1848.

26. Martin, untitled contribution in Armitage, p. 8.

27. Munro, *Arts,* p. 499. Valéry, *Degas,* passim.

29. Denby, *Dancers,* p. 175; Straus, p. 23.

29. Beardsley, quoted in Noël Carroll, "Post-Modern Dance and Expression," in Fancher and Myers, p. 95.

32. Krasovskaya, "Marius Petipa," p. 24; Fokine, "The New Ballet," in Cohen, *Theatre Art,* p. 103.

33. Graham, "A Modern Dancer's Primer for Action," in Rogers, p. 178.

34. Brown, "On Chance," p. 17.

34. Rainer, p. 66; Jakobson, "Linguistics and Poetics," in de George, p. 120.

37. Karsavina, p. 85.

37. The reviews from *Novoe Vremya* and *Novosti* are cited Wiley, n.p.; the review from *Russkaya Musikalnaya Gazeta* is in Krasovskaya, *Russkii Baletnye Teatr,* p. 379.

39. Smith, pp. 239–42.

Chapter 3   The Girdle of Venus

45. *Iliad* 14, 190–220; Apuleius, 1, 405.

45–46. *Aenead* 1, 314–405. The graces are discussed in Gombrich, "Botticelli's Mythologies" and in Panovsky, *Studies.*

46. Duncan, *Life,* p. 84.

47. Shaftesbury, 1: 190; Montesquieu, p. 849.

48. Schiller, pp. 185–86; von Kleist, "Puppet Theatre," in de Zoete, pp. 70–71.

48. Knight, pp. 211–12; Reid, 1: 507.

49. Blasis, *The Art of Dancing,* trans. by R. Barton (London: Edward Bull, 1831), p. 52.

50. Schopenhauer, selection from "The World as Will and Idea," trans. by R. B. Haldane and J. Kemp, in Hofstadter and Kuhns, p. 478; Sartre, p. 376.

51. Hogarth, p. 152; Spencer, p. 111; Hogarth, p. 159.

52. Knight, p. 212.

52. Cage, pp. 91–92; Bayer, 2: 269, 294.

53. Alison, p. 437, 38.

55. Cunningham interviewed by Maggie Lewis, *Christian Science Monitor,* 10 May 1979, p. 20.

57. Quoted in Krasovskaya, *Russkii Baletnye Teatr,* p. 391; Karsavina, p. 181.

Chapter 4   The Achieve of, the Mastery of the Thing!

63. Steele, *The Spectator,* no. 466 (1712).

64–65. Eliot, "The Ballet," p. 442.

65. Lowe, p. 99; Straus, p. 23.

66. Arnheim, "Stricture," p. 645.

66. Danto, p. 142; Best, "Aesthetic of Sport," p. 212.

67. Reid, pp. 255, 258.

68. Jowitt, *Village Voice,* 11 September 1978.

68. Mark, "Works of Virtuosity," p. 42.

70. Adams and Taylor interviewed by Jennifer Dunning, *New York Times,* 26 April 1981.

71. Banes, p. 211.

71. Siegel, *Watching,* p. 133; Croce, p. 425; Bullough, p. 104.

76–77. Volynsky, pp. 47–48; Valéry, "Eupalinos, or The Architect," in *Dialogues,* p. 68.

Chapter 5   What Does the "Dance of the Sugar Plum Fairy" Mean?

83–84. The version of the "Dance of the Sugar Plum Fairy" described here is the one that I recall from various Ballet Russe productions of the 1940s, which seems to be practically identical with the one authorized by Alicia Markova for publication in Labanotation by the Dance Notation Bureau in 1957. To what extent this resembles the original Ivanov choreography I dare not say.

84–85. Langer, *Feeling,* pp. 175, 182; *Problems,* p. 7.

86. Collingwood, p. 274.

87. Augustine, selection from *De Musica,* trans. by W. F. Jackson Knight, in Hofstadter and Kuhns, pp. 185–202, passim.

87–88.   Goodman, *Languages,* pp. 64–65.

88.   Beaujoyeulx, in Cohen, *Theatre Art,* p. 30.

90.   Grigorovich, cited in Balanchine and Mason, p. 316.

92.   Armelagos and Sirridge, "In's and Out's," p. 19; Denby, *Dancers,* pp. 119–20.

92.   Cunningham, pp. 47, 53.

93.   Cunningham, p. 11; Brown, untitled contribution in Cunningham, p. 35.

93.   Reitz, Program, Dance Theatre Workshop, New York, 20–22 March 1980.

96.   Arnheim, *Art,* pp. 363–64, 368, 371.

97.   Matejka, p. 384.

98.   Wynne, "Complaisance," p. 25.

99–100.   Buckle, "Critics' Sabbath," *Ballet* 7, nos. 9–10 (1950): 7–9.

100–101.   Denby, *Looking,* pp. 10–11; *Dancers,* pp. 185, 190.

102.   Symons, "Ballet," p. 66.

Chapter 6   *Verbs of Motion*

110–11.   Langer, *Problems,* pp. 4–6, 8; *Feeling,* p. 186.

111–12.   Sheets-Johnstone, "On Movement," pp. 44, 45.

116.   Taylor, "Down with Choreography," in Cohen, *Modern Dance,* p. 92.

116.   Makarova, p. 113; Taylor, p. 100.

117.   Rosen, *Classical Style,* p. 21.

117–18.   Goodman, *Ways,* p. 40.

118.   Eliot, "Dialogue," p. 34.

119.   Kirstein, "What Ballet Is," pp. 22, 6–7; Martin, p. 212; Kirstein, "Ballet Alphabet," p. 20.

120.   Volynsky, p. 18.

123.   Levinson, in Cohen, *Theatre Art,* p. 116.

123.   Valéry, "Dance and the Soul," p. 38; Levinson, ibid.

123.   Kirstein, "What Ballet Is," p. 32.

123–24.   Violette Verdy, "Speaking of Nureyev," *BR* 5, no. 2: 47.

125.   Wigman, *Book,* pp. 28, 30; Winslow, "A Dancer's Critique of Dance," in Rogers, p. 85.

126.   Kirstein, "What Ballet Is," p. 53; Limón, "An American Accent," in Cohen, *Modern Dance,* p. 20.

127.   Kisselgoff, *New York Times,* 24 August 1975.
Cohen, *Modern Dance,* p. 20.   127.   Kisselgoff, *New York Times,* 24 August 1975.

127.   Taylor interviewed by Deborah Jowitt, *Village Voice,* 23 April 1979; Dean interviewed by John Gruen on "The Sound of Dance," WNCN, New York, 11 May 1980; Bruhn, quoted in John Gruen, *Erik Bruhn* (New York: Viking, 1979), p. 218.

128. Driver interviewed by Jack Anderson, *New York Times,* 25 February 1979.

129. Banes, "'Drive,' She Said: The Dance of Molissa Fenley," in Kirby, "Dance/Movement," p. 14.

129–30. I have used Jowitt's apt remark a number of times, but neither of us can now remember exactly when it appeared in the *Village Voice.*

130. Dunning, *New York Times,* 11 February 1980.

131. Heppenstall, pp. 145, 113, 195; Levin, "Balanchine's Formalism," p. 30.

132. Croce, untitled contribution in Cunningham, p. 25.

133. Vaughan, "Ashton vs. Cunningham?" *Dancing Times* (August 1979), p. 707.

Chapter 7 Lebedinoe Ozero *by Any Other Name*

139–40. Croce, p. 116.

141. Rosen, "Should Music be Played," p. 58.

144. The films were viewed in the Dance Collection, The New York Public Library.

144–45. Bournonville, p. 346.

147. Cunningham interviewed by Allen Robertson, *Ballet News* (January–February 1980): 12–13.

148. King interviewed by John Howell, *Performing Arts Journal* 3, no. 2 (1978): 21.

149. Margolis, "Autographic Nature," p. 424.

149. Armelagos and Sirridge, "Identity Crisis," p. 131, 133.

150. Siegel, *Shapes,* p. 140.

151. Bjørn, p. 21.

152. Bruhn, p. 14.

156–57. "Swine Lake." Danced by Rudolf Nureyev and Graham Fletcher, "The Muppet Show," wcbs-tv, New York, 23 January 1978; Allen, p. 21.

157. Krasovskaya, *Stati,* p. 251.

158. Goldner in Balanchine and Mason, p. 615.

159–60. Harris, pp. 23–25.

161. All the poems quoted are from *The Collected Poems of W. B. Yeats* (New York, Macmillan, 1944). "Daughters of the swan . . . scare a bird" is from "Among School Children"; "Go Pluck Athena . . . dreaming eye" from "Michael Robartes and the Dancer"; "outdanced thought . . ." from "The Double Vision of Michael Robartes"; "mysterious . . . mind" from "The Wild Swans at Coole"; "labour . . . dance" from "Among School Children."

162. Farrell, quoted in Daniel, p. 6.

Bibliography

All the items listed here belong to one of three categories: works that I have used substantially in preparing this book; works that I have not drawn on directly but have found generally interesting and provocative in relation to the issues considered; works that deal specifically with these issues and that I have consequently consulted though I have made little use of them. Any of these, of course, may be of interest to the reader.

Theoretical discussions of dance tend to lurk in unlikely places and sometimes emerge from discussions of another subject entirely, which accounts for some of the apparently impertinent titles. Several of the items never mention dance at all, though they are concerned with problems—such as the nature of performance—that are applicable to dance. Some of the latter were among my happiest discoveries, and they form an important part of the bibliography, because they raise questions that have not been treated in books that deal exclusively with dance.

My special thanks to the Institute for Scientific Information's *Current Contents*, which I peruse weekly and which led me to some of the most interesting listings in this bibliography.

Alison, Archibald. *Essays on the Nature and Principles of Taste.* Edinburgh: J. J. G. and G. Robinson; and Bell and Bradfute, 1790.

Allen, Woody. "A Guide to Some of the Lesser Ballets." In *Without Feathers*, pp. 18–23. New York: Warner Books, 1975.

Anderson, Jack. "Ferment and Controversy." *Dance Magazine*, August 1969, pp. 47–55.

————. "Idealists, Materialists and the Thirty-two Fouettés." *BR* 5, no. 1 (1975–76): 13–22.

Anonymous. "La Danse chez les imaginaires." *Revue d'esthétique* 6 (1953): 244–64.

Aristotle. *Poetics*. Translated by Ingram Bywater. *Politics*. Book 8. Translated by B. Jowett. In *The Basic Works*. Edited by Richard McKeon. New York: Random House, 1941.

Armelagos, Adina, and Mary Sirridge. "The Identity Crisis in Dance." *JAAC* 37 (1978): 129–39.

————. "The In's and Out's of Dance: Expression as an Aspect of Style." *JAAC* 36 (1977): 15–24.

Armitage, Merle, ed. *Martha Graham*. Los Angeles: Armitage, 1937.

Arnheim, Rudolf. *Art and Visual Perception*. Berkeley: University of California Press, 1954.

————. "Psychology of the Dance." *Dance Magazine*, August 1946, pp. 20, 38–39.

————. "A Stricture on Space and Time." *Critical Inquiry* 4 (1978): 645–55.

Aschengreen, Erik. "The Beautiful Danger: Facets of the Romantic Ballet." Translated by Patricia N. McAndrew. *DP* 58 (1974).

Bachelard, Gaston. *The Poetics of Space*. Translated by Maria Jolas. New York: Orion Press, 1964.

Baker, Carlos. "Moralist and Hedonist: Emerson, Henry Adams, and the Dance." *New England Quarterly* 52 (1979): 27–37.

Balanchine, George, and Francis Mason. *Balanchine's Complete Stories of the Great Ballets*. Garden City, N.Y.: Doubleday, 1977.

Banes, Sally. *Terpsichore in Sneakers: Post-Modern Dance*. Boston: Houghton Mifflin, 1980.

Barfield, Owen. *Poetic Diction: A Study in Meaning*. 3d ed. Middletown, Conn.: Wesleyan University Press, 1973.

Barko, Carol. "The Dancer and the Becoming of Language." *Yale French Studies* 54 (1977): 173–87.

Baron, A. *Lettres à Sophie sur la danse*. Paris: Dondey-Dupré, 1825.

Bartenieff, Irmgard, Martha Davis, and Forrestine Paulay. *Four Adaptations of Effort Theory in Research and Teaching*. New York: Dance Notation Bureau, 1970.

Baryshnikov, Mikhail. *Baryshnikov at Work*. New York: Knopf, 1976.

Batteux, Charles. *Les Beaux Arts réduits à un même principe*. Paris: Durand, 1746.

Battock, Gregory, ed. *Minimal Art: A Critical Anthology*. New York: Dutton, 1968.

Bayer, Raymond. *L'Esthétique de la grâce: introduction à l'étude des équilibres de structure.* 2 vols. Paris: Félix Alcan, 1933.

Beardsley, Monroe C. *Aesthetics: Problems in the Philosophy of Criticism.* New York: Harcourt, 1958.

―――. "What is Going on in a Dance?" Paper delivered at Illuminating Dance Conference, Temple University, Philadelphia, April 1979.

Beaumont, Cyril W. *The Ballet Called Swan Lake.* London: C. W. Beaumont, 1952.

Beiswanger, George. "Chance and Design in Choreography." *JAAC* 21 (1962): 13–17.

―――. "Doing and Viewing Dances: A Perspective for the Practice of Criticism." *DP* 55 (1973): 7–13.

Bell, Clive. *Art* [1914]. New ed. New York: G. P. Putnam, 1958.

Bergson, Henri. *Time and Free Will: An Essay on the Immediate Data of Consciousness.* Translated by F. L. Pogson. London, George Allen and Unwin, Ltd., 1959.

Berleant, Arnold. *The Aesthetic Field: A Phenomenology of Aesthetic Experience.* Springfield, Ill.: Charles C. Thomas, 1969.

Bertrand, Monique, and Mathilde Dumont. *Expression corporelle: mouvement et pensée.* Paris: J. Vrin, 1970.

Best, David. "The Aesthetic of Sport." *BJA* 14 (1974): 197–213.

―――. *Expression in Movement and the Arts: A Philosophical Enquiry.* London: Lepus, 1974.

―――. *Philosophy and Human Movement.* London: Unwin, 1978.

Bjørn, Dinna. "On Dancing Bournonville." Special issue of the *Danish Journal,* pp. 20–23. Published by the Ministry of Foreign Affairs of Denmark [1979].

Bouissac, Paul. *Circus and Culture: A Semiotic Approach.* Bloomington, Ind.: Indiana University Press, 1976.

―――. *La Mesure des gestes.* The Hague: Mouton, 1973.

Bournonville, August. *My Theatre Life.* Translated by Patricia N. McAndrew. Middletown, Conn.: Wesleyan University Press, 1979.

Brillant, Maurice. *Problèmes de la danse.* Paris: Armand Colin, 1953.

Brown, Carolyn. "McLuhan and the Dance." *BR* 1, no. 4 (1966): 13–20.

―――. "On Chance." *BR* 2, no. 2 (1968): 7–25.

Brown, Estelle T. "Toward a Structuralist Approach to Ballet: 'Swan Lake' and 'The White Haired Girl.'" *Western Humanities Review* 32 (1978): 227–40.

Brown, Trisha, and Yvonne Rainer. "A Conversation about 'Glacial Decoy.'" *October* 10 (1980): 29–37.

Bruhn, Erik. "Beyond Technique." *DP* 36 (1968).

Buckle, Richard. "Abstract Ballet." *Ballet* 4, no. 5 (1947): 20–24.

―――. *Buckle at the Ballet.* New York: Atheneum, 1980.

Bullough, Edward. *Aesthetics: Lectures and Essays.* Edited by Elizabeth M. Wilkinson. Stanford, Calif.: Stanford University Press, 1957.

178 / *Next Week, Swan Lake*

Burke, Edmund. *A Philosophical Enquiry into the Origins of our Ideas of the Sublime and the Beautiful* [1757]. London: Routledge and Kegan Paul, 1958.
Cage, John. "Grace and Clarity." In *Silence*, pp. 89–93. Middletown, Conn.: Wesleyan University Press, 1961.
Cahusac, Louis de. *La Danse ancienne et moderne*. 3 vols. La Haye: J. Neaulme, 1754.
Campbell, Joseph. "Symbolism and the Dance." *Dance Observer*, 1950, February, pp. 20–23; March, pp. 36–37; April, pp. 52–53.
Carandente, Giovanni. "Il Balletto come Fatto Visuale." *Galleria* 9 (1959): 231–36.
Cassirer, Ernst. *Philosophy of Symbolic Forms*. Translated by Ralph Manheim. Vol. 2. New Haven: Yale University Press, 1955.
Chartier, Emile [Alain]. *Système des beaux-arts*. Paris: Gallimard, 1926.
————. *Vingt leçons sur les beaux-arts*. Paris: Gallimard, 1931.
Christout, Marie-Françoise. "L'Oeuvre et l'interprète: problèmes de la création chorégraphique." *Revue d'esthétique* 9 (1956): 401–20.
Chujoy, Anatole. "Russian Balletomania." *Dance Index* 7, no. 3 (1948).
Cohen, Selma Jeanne. "Avant-Garde Choreography." *Criticism* 3(1961): 16–35.
————. "Bournonville and the Question of Preservation." *Dance Magazine*, November 1979, pp. 77–78.
————, ed. *Dance as a Theatre Art: Source Readings in Dance History*. New York: Harper & Row, 1974.
————. *Doris Humphrey: An Artist First*. Middletown, Conn.: Wesleyan University Press, 1972.
————. "In Search of Satanella." *Dance Research Journal* 11 (1979): 25–30.
————. "A Prolegomenon to an Aesthetics of Dance." *JAAC* 21 (1962): 19–26.
————, ed. *The Modern Dance: Seven Statements of Belief*. Middletown, Conn.: Wesleyan University Press, 1965.
Collingwood, Robin George. *The Principles of Art*. Oxford: Clarendon Press, 1938.
Courtney, Richard. "Drama and Aesthetics." *BJA* 8 (1968): 373–86.
Crane, R. S., ed. *Critics and Criticism*. Chicago: University of Chicago Press, 1952.
Croce, Arlene. *Afterimages*. New York: Knopf, 1977.
Cunningham, Merce et al. "Time to Walk in Space." *DP* 34 (1968).
Daniel, David. "A Conversation with Suzanne Farrell." *BR* 7, no. 1 (1978–79): 1–15.
Danto, Arthur C. "The Transfiguration of the Commonplace." *JAAC* 33 (1964): 139–48.
Davies, Douglas. "Post-Everything." *Art in America* 68, no. 2 (1980): 11–13.
Davies, Sir John. *Orchestra or a Poem of Dancing* [1596]. Brooklyn: Dance Horizons, 1977.

De George, Richard T., and Fernande M., eds. *The Structuralists*. Garden City, N.Y.: Doubleday, 1972.

Denby, Edwin. *Looking at the Dance*. New York: Pellegrini & Cudahy, 1949.

————. *Dancers, Buildings and People in the Streets*. New York: Horizon, 1965.

Dickie, George. *Art and the Aesthetic: An Institutional Analysis*. Ithaca, N.Y.: Cornell University Press, 1974.

————. "Art Narrowly and Broadly Speaking." *American Philosophical Quarterly* 5 (1968): 71–77.

Diderot, Denis. "Entretiens sur 'Le Fils Naturel'" [1757]. In *Oeuvres esthétiques*, pp. 71–175. Edited by Paul Vernière. Paris: Editions Garniers Frères, 1959.

Dipert, Randall R. "The Composer's Intentions: An Examination of their Relevance for Performance." *Musical Quarterly* 66 (1980): 205–18.

Dubos, Jean Baptiste, Abbé. *Réflexions critiques sur la poésie et sur la peinture*. 2 vols. Paris: J. Mariette, 1719.

Dufrenne, Mikel. *The Phenomenology of Aesthetic Experience* [1953]. Translated by Edward S. Casey et al. Evanston, Ill.: Northwestern University Press, 1973.

Dumont, Léon. *Le Sentiment du gracieux*. Paris: Auguste Durand, 1863.

Duncan, Isadora. *The Art of the Dance*. New York: Theatre Arts, 1928.

————. *My Life*. New York: Liveright, 1927.

Durgnat, Raymond. "Rock, Rhythm and Dance." *BJA* 11 (1971): 28–47.

Edie, James M. "Appearance and Reality: An Essay on the Philosophy of the Theater." *Philosophy and Literature* 4 (1980): 3–17.

Eisenberg, Emanuel. "The Meaning of Dance." *Trend*, May–June 1934, pp. 105–11.

Eliot, T. S. "The Ballet." *The Criterion* 3 (1925): 441–43.

————. "A Dialogue on Dramatic Poetry." In *Selected Essays 1917–1932*, pp. 31–45. New York: Harcourt, 1932.

Ellis, Havelock. *The Dance of Life*. Boston: Houghton Mifflin, 1923.

Elsbree, Langdon. "The Purest and Most Perfect Form of Play: Some Novelists and the Dance." *Criticism* 14 (1972): 361–72.

Fancher, Gordon, and Gerald Myers, eds. *Philosophical Essays on Dance*. Brooklyn: Dance Horizons, 1981.

Feibleman, James K. "On the Metaphysics of the Performing Arts." *JAAC* 29 (1970): 295–99.

Forti, Simone. *Handbook in Motion*. New York: New York University Press, 1974.

Friesen, Joanna. "Perceiving Dance." *Journal of Aesthetic Education* 9 (1975): 97–108.

Gautier, Théophile. *The Romantic Ballet as Seen by Théophile Gautier*. Edited by Cyril W. Beaumont. Rev. ed. London: C. W. Beaumont, 1947.

Gibbons, T. H. "The Reverend Stewart Headlam and the Emblematic Dancer: 1877–1894." *BJA* 5 (1965): 329–40.

Gilson, Etienne. *Forms and Substances in the Arts.* Translated by Salvator Attanasio. New York: Scribner's, 1966.

Giudici, Nicolas. "Philosophie et virtuosité." *Critique,* October 1979, pp. 869–74.

Gombrich, E. H. *Art and Illusion: A Study in the Psychology of Pictorial Representation.* New York: Pantheon, 1956.

――――. "Botticelli's Mythologies: A Study in the Neoplatonic Symbolism of His Circle." *Journal of the Warburg and Courtauld Institutes* 7 (1945): 7–60.

――――. "Moment and Movement in Art." *Journal of the Warburg and Courtauld Institutes* 27 (1964): 293–306.

Goodman, Nelson. *Languages of Art.* Indianapolis, Ind.: Bobbs-Merrill, 1968.

――――. *Ways of Worldmaking.* Indianapolis, Ind.: Hackett, 1978.

Gouhier, Henri. *L'Essence du théâtre.* Paris: Plon, 1943.

Greene, Gordon K. "For Whom and Why Does the Composer Prepare a Score?" *JAAC* 33 (1974): 503–8.

Greene, Theodore M. *The Arts and the Art of Criticism.* Princeton, N.J.: Princeton University Press, 1940.

Greimas, A. J., R. Jakobsón et al. *Sign, Language, Culture.* The Hague: Mouton, 1970.

Hammond, Phillip and Sandra N. "The Internal Logic of Dance: A Weberian Perspective on the History of Ballet." *Journal of Social History* 12 (1979): 591–608.

Harris, James. "A Dialogue Concerning Art" [1744]. In *The Works of James Harris,* vol. 1, pp. 1–30. London: Wingrave, 1801.

Harrison, Nigel. "Creativity in Musical Performance." *BJA* 18 (1978): 300–306.

Hein, Hilde. "Performance as an Aesthetic Category." *JAAC* 29 (1970): 381–86.

Heppenstall, Rayner. *Apology for Dancing.* London: Faber & Faber, 1936.

Hofmann, Wilfried A. "Of Beauty and the Dance: Toward an Aesthetics of Ballet." *DP* 55 (1973): 15–27.

Hofstadter, Albert, and Richard Kuhns, eds. *Philosophies of Art and Beauty.* Chicago: University of Chicago Press, 1976.

Hogarth, William. *The Analysis of Beauty* [1753]. Edited by Joseph T. A. Burke. Oxford: Clarendon Press, 1953.

Hume, David. *An Enquiry Concerning the Principles of Morals.* London: A. Millar, 1751.

Humphrey, Doris. *The Art of Making Dances.* Edited by Barbara Pollack. New York: Rinehart, 1959.

Ingarden, Roman. *The Literary Work of Art.* Translated by George G. Grabowicz. Evanston, Ill.: Northwestern University Press, 1973.

Institute for Theatre Research. *Theatre Research Studies* 2. Copenhagen: University of Copenhagen, 1972.

Jaffe, Judith Snyder. "The Expressive Meaning of a Dance." *JAAC* 12 (1954): 518–22.

Jowitt, Deborah. *Dance Beat: Selected Views and Reviews 1967–1976.* New York: Dekker, 1977.

Kaeppler, Adrienne L. "Dance as Myth—Myth as Dance: A Challenge to Traditional Viewpoints." Paper delivered at the Asian and Pacific Dance Conference, University of Hawaii, Honolulu, August 1978.

Kames, Henry Home, Lord. *Elements of Criticism.* 3 vols. Edinburgh: A. Kincaid & J. Bell, 1762.

Karsavina, Tamara. *Theatre Street.* New York: Dutton, 1931.

Katz, Ruth. "The Egalitarian Waltz." *Comparative Studies in Society and History* 6 (1973): 368–77.

Kennick, W. E., ed. *Art and Philosophy: Readings in Aesthetics.* 2d ed. New York: St. Martin's Press, 1979.

Kermode, Frank. *Romantic Image.* London: Routledge and Kegan Paul, 1957.

Khatchadourian, Haig. "Movement and Action in the Performing Arts." *JAAC* 37 (1978): 25–36.

Kirby, Michael. *The Art of Time: Essays on the Avant-Garde.* New York: Dutton, 1969.

———, ed. "The New Dance." *The Drama Review* 16 (1972): 115–50.

———, ed. "Post-Modern Dance." *The Drama Review* 19 (1975): 3–77.

———, ed. "Dance/Movement." *The Drama Review* 24 (1980): 2–102.

Kirstein, Lincoln. *Movement and Metaphor.* New York: Praeger, 1970.

———. "Ballet Alphabet" [1939] and "What Ballet is About" [1959]. In *Three Pamphlets Collected.* Brooklyn: Dance Horizons, 1967.

Kivy, Peter. *The Corded Shell: Reflections on Musical Expression.* Princeton: Princeton University Press, 1980.

Knight, Richard Payne. *An Analytical Inquiry into the Principles of Taste.* 4th ed. London: Luke Hansard, 1808.

Kostelanetz, Richard, ed. *Esthetics Contemporary.* Buffalo, N.Y.: Prometheus, 1978.

Kowzan, Tadeusz. "The Sign in the Theater." *Diogenes* 61 (1968): 52–80.

———. "Music and the Plastic Arts in the Conquest of Space and Time." *Diogenes* 64 (1971): 1–20.

Krasovskaya, Vera. "Marius Petipa and 'The Sleeping Beauty.'" *DP* 49 (1972).

———. *Russkii Baletnye Teatr vtoroi poloviny XIX veka* [Russian Ballet Theatre of the Second Half of the Nineteenth Century]. Leningrad/Moscow: Iskusstvo, 1963.

———. *Stati o balete* [Articles about Ballet]. Leningrad: Iskusstvo, 1967.

Kristeller, Paul Oskar. "The Modern System of the Arts." *Journal of the History of Ideas* 12 (1951): 496–527; 13 (1952): 17–46.

Laban, Rudolf. *Choreutics.* Edited by Lisa Ullmann. London: Macdonald and Evans, 1966.

———. *The Mastery of Movement* [1950]. Edited and revised by Lisa Ullmann. Boston: Plays, Inc., 1975.

Lang, Berel, ed. *The Concept of Style.* Philadelphia: University of Pennsylvania Press, 1979.

Langer, Susanne K. *Feeling and Form.* New York: Scribner's, 1953.

———. *Problems of Art.* New York: Scribner's, 1957.

———, ed. *Reflections on Art: A Source Book of Writings by Artists, Critics, and Philosophers.* Baltimore: Johns Hopkins University Press, 1958.

Levin, David Michael. "Balanchine's Formalism." *DP* 55 (1973): 30–47.

———. "The Embodiment of Performance." *Salmagundi*, Nos. 31–32 (1975–76), pp. 120–42.

———. "Philosophers and the Dance." *BR* 6, no. 2 (1977): 71–78.

———. "The Spacing of Comedy and Tragedy: A Phenomenological Study of Perception." *Journal of the British Society for Phenomenology* 11 (1980): 16–36.

Levinson, André. "The Idea of the Dance from Aristotle to Mallarmé." *Theatre Arts*, August 1927, pp. 571–83.

Levinson, Jerrold. "What a Musical Work Is." *Journal of Philosophy* 77 (1980): 5–28.

Lindberg, Mary Klinger. "A Delightful Play upon the Eye: William Hogarth and Theatrical Dance." *Dance Chronicle* 4 (1981): 19–45.

Livet, Anne, ed. *Contemporary Dance.* New York: Abbeville Press, 1978.

Lopukhov, Fyodor. "Annals of 'The Sleeping Beauty.'" *BR* 5, no. 4 (1975–76): 21–35.

Lowe, Benjamin. *The Beauty of Sport: A Cross-Disciplinary Inquiry.* Englewood Cliffs, N.J.: Prentice-Hall, 1977.

Lucian. "On Pantomime." In *The Works of Lucian of Samosata.* Translated by H. W. and F. G. Fowler. Oxford: Clarendon Press, 1905.

McGrath, Robert L. "The Dance as Pictorial Metaphor." *Gazette des beaux-arts* 89 (1977): 81–92.

Makarova, Natalia. *A Dance Autobiography.* New York: Knopf, 1980.

Malek, James S. *The Arts Compared: An Aspect of Eighteenth-Century British Aesthetics.* Detroit: Wayne State University Press, 1974.

Mallarmé, Stéphane. *Oeuvres complètes.* Edited by Henri Mondor and G. Jean-Aubry. Paris: Gallimard, 1956.

Margolis, Joseph. *Art and Philosophy.* Brighton, Sussex: Harvester, 1980.

———. "The Autographic Nature of the Dance." *JAAC* 39 (1981): 419–27.

———. *The Language of Art and Art Criticism.* Detroit: Published for the University of Cincinnati by Wayne State University Press, 1965.

———, ed. *Philosophy Looks at the Arts.* Rev. ed. Philadelphia: Temple University Press, 1978.

Mark, Thomas Carson. "On Works of Virtuosity." *Journal of Philosophy* 77 (1980): 28–45.

———. "Philosophy of Piano Playing: Reflections on the Concept of Performance." *Philosophy and Phenomenological Research* 41, no. 3 (1981): 299–324.

Martin, John. *Introduction to the Dance.* New York: W. W. Norton, 1939.

Matejka, Ladislav, and Irwin R. Titunik. *Semiotics of Art: Prague School Contributions*. Cambridge: MIT Press, 1976.

Menestrier, Claude François. *Des Ballets anciens et modernes selon les règles du théâtre*. Paris: Guignard, 1862.

Merleau-Ponty, Maurice. *Phenomenology of Perception*. Translated by Colin Smith. London: Routledge and Kegan Paul, 1962.

Michel, Artur. "The Ballet d'action before Noverre." *Dance Index* 6 (1947): 52–72.

Monahan, James. *The Nature of Ballet: A Critic's Reflections*. London: Pitman, 1976.

Montesquieu, Charles-Louis de Secondat, baron de la Brede et de. "Essai sur le goût" [1757]. In *Oeuvres complètes*, pp. 845–52. [Edited by] Daniel Oster. Paris: Editions du Seuil, 1964.

Munro, Thomas. "'The Afternoon of a Faun' and the Interrelation of the Arts." *JAAC* 10 (1951): 95–111.

———. *The Arts and their Interrelations*. New York: Liberal Arts, 1949.

Murphy, Patricia. "Ballet Reform in Mid-Eighteenth-Century France: The *Philosophes* and Noverre." *Symposium* 30 (1976): 27–41.

Nietzsche, Friedrich. *The Birth of Tragedy* [1886] and *The Case of Wagner* [1888] . 2 vols. in 1. Translated by Walter Kaufmann. New York: Vintage, 1967.

Noverre, Jean Georges. *Letters on Dancing and Ballets* [1760]. Translated by C. W. Beaumont from the rev. and enlarged ed. published at St. Petersburg, 1803. London: C. W. Beaumont, 1951.

O'Grady, Terence J. "Interpretive Freedom and the Composer-Performer Relationship." *Journal of Aesthetic Education* 14 (1980): 55–67.

Ortega y Gasset, José. *The Dehumanization of Art* [1925]. Translated by Helene Weyl. Princeton, N.J.: Princeton University Press, 1948.

Panofsky, Erwin. *Meaning in the Visual Arts*. Garden CIty, N.Y.: Doubleday, 1955.

———. *Renaissance and Renascences in Western Art*. Stockholm: Almquist and Wiksell, 1960.

———. *Studies in Iconology: Humanistic Themes in the Art of the Renaissance*. New York: Oxford University Press, 1939.

Pauly, Herta. "Inside Kabuki: An Experience in Comparative Aesthetics." *JAAC* 25 (1967): 293–305.

Percival, John, and Noel Goodwin. "Toward the Source of Swan Lake." *Dance and Dancers*, June 1977, pp. 22–27.

Petipa, Marius. *Materialy, vospomenaniya, stati* [Documents, Memoirs, Articles] Edited by Yury Slonimsky. Leningrad: Iskusstvo, 1971.

Philipson, Morris, ed. *Aesthetics Today*. Cleveland: Meridian-World, 1961.

Plato. *Laws*, Books 2 and 7. *Republic*, Book 3. In *The Dialogues of Plato*. Translated by B. Jowett. 2 vols. New York: Random House, 1937.

Pops, Martin L., ed. "Special Dance Issue." *Salmagundi*, nos. 33–34 (1976).

Prudhommeau, Germaine. "L'Erotisme et la danse." *Revue d'esthétique* 21 (1978): 277–85.

———. "L'Espace chorégraphique." *Sciences de l'art* 4 (1967): 103–13.

Pure, Michel de. *Idée des spectacles ancien et nouveaux*. Paris: Michel Brunet, 1668.

Rainer, Yvonne. *Work 1961–73*. New York: New York University Press, 1974.

Rawson, C. J. "Gentlemen and Dancing Masters." In *Henry Fielding and the Augustan Ideal under Stress*, pp. 3–34. London: Routledge and Kegan Paul, 1972.

Redfern, R. B. "Rudolf Laban and the Aesthetics of Dance." *BJA* 16 (1976): 61–67.

Reid, Louis Arnaud. "Sport, the Aesthetic and Art." *British Journal of Educational Studies* 18 (1970): 245–58.

Reid, Thomas. "Essay on the Intellectual Powers of Man" [1785]. In *Philosophical Works*, vol. 1, pp. 215–508. [Edited by] Sir William Hamilton. Hildesheim: G. Olms, 1967.

Rémond de Saint Mard, Toussaint. *Réflexions sur l'opéra*. La Haye: J. Neaulme, 1741.

Reynolds, Sir Joshua. *Discourses on Art* [1769–91]. Chicago: Packard, 1945.

Reynolds, Nancy. *Repertory in Review: 40 Years of the New York City Ballet*. New York: Dial, 1977.

Ricoeur, Paul. *Freedom and Nature: The Voluntary and the Involuntary*. Translated by Erazím Kohák. Evanston, Ill.: Northwestern University Press, 1966.

Robertson, Thomas. *An Inquiry into the Fine Arts*. London: W. Strahan and T. Cadell, 1784.

Rogers, Frederick Rand, ed. *Dance: A Basic Educational Technique*. New York: Macmillan, 1941.

Rosen, Charles. *The Classical Style: Haydn, Mozart, Beethoven*. New York: W. W. Norton, 1972.

———. "Should Music be Played Wrong?" *High Fidelity*, May 1971, pp. 55–58.

Sartre, Jean-Paul. *Being and Nothingness* [1943]. Translated by Hazel Barnes. London: Methuen, 1969.

Schiller, Friedrich. "On Grace and Dignity" [c. 1795–1801]. In *Essays Aesthetical and Philosophical*, pp. 168–223. Translated anonymous. London: George Bell, 1875.

Shaftesbury, Anthony Ashley Cooper, Earl of. *Characteristics of Men, Manners, Opinions, Times*. 2d ed. London: n.p., 1714.

Sheets-Johnstone, Maxine. "An Account of Recent Changes in Dance in the U.S.A." *Leonardo* 11 (1978): 197–201.

———. "On Movement and Objects in Motion: The Phenomenology of the Visible in Dance." *Journal of Aesthetic Education* 13 (1979): 33–46.

Shelton, Suzanne. *Divine Dancer: A Biography of Ruth St. Denis*. Garden City, N.Y.: Doubleday, 1981.

Siegel, Marcia B. *At the Vanishing Point: A Critic Looks at Dance.* New York: Saturday Review Books, 1972.

————. *The Shapes of Change: Images of American Dance.* Boston: Houghton Mifflin, 1979.

————. *Watching the Dance Go By.* Boston: Houghton Mifflin, 1977.

Sircello, Guy. *Mind & Art: An Essay on the Varieties of Expression.* Princeton: Princeton University Press, 1972.

————. *A New Theory of Beauty.* Princeton: Princeton University Press, 1975.

Slonimsky, Yury. "Writings on Lev Ivanov." Translated by Anatole Chujoy. *DP* 2 (1959).

Smith, Adam. "On the Nature of that Imitation Which Takes Place in What Are Called the Imitative Arts." In *Essays on Philosophical Subjects.* pp. 179–252. London: T. Cadell, Jr. & W. Davies, 1795.

Souriau, Etienne. *La Correspondance des arts.* Paris: Flammarion, 1969.

Souriau, Paul. *L'Esthétique du mouvement.* Paris: F. Alcan, 1889.

Sparshott, Francis. "On the Question: Why Do Philosophers Neglect the Aesthetics of the Dance: Considerations in Anticipation of an Inquiry." Paper delivered at the Pacific Division Conference of the American Society for Aesthetics, Pacific Grove, California, April 1980.

Spence, Joseph. *Crito: Or, A Dialogue on Beauty.* London: R. Dodsley, 1752.

Spencer, Herbert. "Gracefulness" [1852]. In *Essays: Moral, Political and Aesthetic,* pp. 107–13. New York: Philosophical Library, 1957.

Stokes, Adrian. "Form in Art: A Psychoanalytic Interpretation." *JAAC* 18 (1959): 193–203.

————. *Tonight the Ballet.* London: Faber and Faber, 1934.

Straus, Erwin. *Phenomenological Psychology.* Translated by Erling Eng. New York: Basic Books, 1966.

Strauss, G. B. "The Aesthetics of Dominance." *JAAC* 37 (1978): 73–79.

Symons, Arthur. "Ballet, Pantomime, and Poetic Drama." *The Dome* 1 (1898): 65–71.

————. "Dancing as Soul Expression." *The Forum,* October 1921, pp. 308–17.

Thiess, Frank. *Der Tanz als Kunstwerk.* 3d ed. Munich: Delphin-Verlag, 1923.

Thomas, Carolyn E., ed. *Aesthetics and Dance.* Reston, Va.: American Alliance for Health, Physical Education, Recreation and Dance, 1980.

Valéry, Paul. "Dance and the Soul" ["L'Ame et la danse," 1925]. In *Dialogues.* Translated by William McCausland Stewart. Bollingen Series 45, vol. 4, pp. 25–62. Edited by Jackson Mathews. New York: Pantheon, 1956.

————. "Degas Dance Drawing" [1935–38]. In *Degas Manet Morisot.* Translated by David Paul. Bollingen Series 45, vol. 12, pp. 1–102. Edited by Jackson Mathews. New York: Pantheon, 1960.

Van Camp, Julie. "Anti-Geneticism and Critical Practice in Dance." *Dance Research Journal* 13 (1980): 29–35.

Vaughan, David. *Frederick Ashton and his Ballets*. New York: Knopf, 1977.

Véron, Eugène. *Aesthetics*. Translated by W. H. Armstrong. London: Chapman and Hale, 1879.

Volynsky, Akim Lvovitch [A. L. Flekser]. *Kniga Likovanii* [Book of Exultation] Leningrad: 1925. Partially translated by Seymour Barofsky as "The Book of Exultation" in *Dance Scope* 5, no. 2 (1971): 16–35, and 6, no. 1 (1972): 46–53.

Wagner, Richard. "Zukunstmusik." In *Richard Wagner's Prose Works*, vol. 3, pp. 293–345. Translated by William Ashton Ellis. London: Kegan Paul, 1894.

Weaver, John. *Essay towards an History of Dancing*. London: J. Tonson, 1712.

Webster, William E. "A Theory of the Compositional Work of Music." *JAAC* 33 (1974): 59–66.

Weiss, Paul. *Nine Basic Arts*. Carbondale, Ill.: Southern Illinois University Press, 1961.

Wertz, S. W. "Are Sports Art Forms?" *Journal of Aesthetic Education* 13 (1979): 107–8.

Whiting, H. T. A., and D. W. Masterson. *Readings in the Aesthetic of Sport*. London: Lepus, 1974.

Wigman, Mary. *The Language of Dance*. Translated by Walter Sorell. Middletown, Conn.: Wesleyan University Press, 1966.

———. *The Mary Wigman Book*. Edited and translated by Walter Sorell. Middletown, Conn.: Wesleyan University Press, 1975.

Wiley, Roland John. "Tchaikovsky's *Swan Lake*: The First Productions in Moscow and St. Petersburg." Ph.D. diss., Harvard University, 1975.

Woodruff, Dianne L. "On Composing a Period Ballet: A Chat with Mary Skeaping." *Dance Scope* 4, no. 2 (1970): 18–25.

Wynne, Shirley. "Complaisance, an Eighteenth-Century Cool." *Dance Scope* 5, no. 1 (1970): 22–36.

———. "From Ballet to Ballroom: Dancing in the Revolutionary Era." *Dance Scope* 10, no. 1 (1975–76): 65–73.

Yasser, Joseph. "The Variation Form and Synthesis of the Arts." *JAAC* 3 (1956): 318–23.

Yates, Frances A. *The French Academies of the Sixteenth Century*. London: The Warburg Institute, University of London, 1947.

———. *Theatre of the World*. London: Routledge and Kegan Paul, 1969.

Zelinger, Jacob. "Semiotics and Theatre Dance." In *New Directions in Dance*, pp. 39–50. Edited by Diana Taplin. Toronto: Pergamon, 1979.

Zoete, Beryl de. *The Thunder and the Freshness*. London: N. Spearman, 1963.

INDEX